Love Your Neighbour
for God's Sake

Love Your Neighbour for God's Sake

Justyn Rees

Hodder & Stoughton
LONDON   SYDNEY   AUCKLAND

Copyright © 1997 by Justyn Rees

First published in Great Britain in 1997

The right of Justyn Rees to be identified as the Author of
the Work has been asserted by him in accordance with the
Copyright, Designs and Patents Act 1988.

1 3 5 7 9 10 8 6 4 2

British Library Cataloguing in Publication Data
A record for this book is available from the British Library

ISBN 0 340 69417 3

Typeset by Palimpsest Book Production Limited
Polmont, Stirlingshire
Printed and bound in Great Britain by
Mackays of Chatham PLC, Chatham, Kent

Hodder and Stoughton Ltd
A division of Hodder Headline PLC
338 Euston Road
London NW1 3BH

To my wife, Joy,
who does it all while
I just write books about it.

Contents

1

An Introduction between Friends

Evangelism is an overture to a relationship, rather than an explanation of a religion

Great-Uncle Willie was tall and gaunt. His black suit and overcoat reinforced the impression of an undertaker, while the determined jut of his jaw, offset by his sunken cheeks, lent the impression that the disposal of the dead was a high calling. But hidden behind his forbidding exterior was a struggle between a shy-natured man who preferred to keep himself to himself, and a determined evangelist who was driven to share the gospel with every stranger he met.

Climbing into the empty compartment of a train one day, he prayed that God would send him a fellow traveller with whom he might share his message. No one joined him. But at the next station in climbed a teenage girl, who nervously took her seat opposite.

The train lurched off and Willie had his captive audience. And captive it was, for the carriage had no connecting corridor. It took him several minutes before he could bring himself to say anything. How was he to start the conversation? What was he to say? How would she react? But he must hurry, for soon the train would reach the next station and she might be gone and he would have failed in his mission. She might then be run over by a truck and be lost to eternal torment!

Meanwhile the girl concentrated on looking out of the window – anything to avoid the stare of the spectre opposite her. Why had she chosen this compartment? How long was it to the next station? Why did he keep staring at her? Then the worst happened.

The man opposite cleared his throat, leant forward and, towering over her, asked in a deep, resonant voice: 'Are you ready to die?'

At that precise moment the train let out a shrill whistle and shot into a tunnel. The girl screamed in the darkness and lunged for the alarm cord hanging over the window. Immediately the brakes locked on and the train slithered to a standstill, half in and half out of the far end of the tunnel.

Fear of embarrassment

Perhaps it's in the genes, but I have inherited my great-uncle's determination to share the gospel. And to cap it all, I am cursed with his shyness. I am a private kind of person who likes to mind my own business. I get embarrassed at the need to communicate with others and the fear of embarrassing them reinforces my plight.

Yet the beauty of the secret that I guard forces me to open my mouth.

So I have done a lot of thinking about how to solve this problem. And despite my retiring nature, I have done a lot of talking with others about it. I am delighted to discover that I am not alone! There are others out there who are as torn apart as I am.

Fear of strangers

One of the big impediments to me and my fellow sufferers is that evangelism is often taught as something we should offer to strangers, people we meet on the street, on the bus, on the plane; people we travel overseas as missionaries to evangelise. I hate talking to strangers!

But what if evangelism was addressed not to strangers but to real people whom we knew, friends, neighbours, relatives? I don't mind having a chat with a friend – in fact there are few joys greater that a tête-à-tête with people with whom I have something in common.

But there are people who would rather talk to strangers, people with whom they have no kind of relationship. A neighbour of mine was a bit like that.

Reinhardt went to Bible college. He didn't go because he wanted to be a pastor or a priest. He had become a Christian in his forties and was determined to make up for lost time. He filled his mind with Hebrew and Greek, with theology and eschatology, homiletics and homilies. But when he came home he couldn't communicate with real people.

Yet Reinhardt was determined to communicate the gospel.

He phoned me one day. 'Justyn, I have a wonderful idea for how to evangelise our whole town.'

'What's that, Reinhardt?'

'Well, we need to address needy people, just like Jesus did. We should find out all the people who are new arrivals in the community, send them a letter of welcome and then go to visit them. Likewise we should find out all the people who are just out of hospital, send them a card and follow up with a visit. We could do something similar for single parents, immigrants, ex-prisoners . . .' The list went on and on.

'How in the world are we going to find all these names, let alone the addresses?'

'Well, Justyn, you are an evangelist. You should be able to find a way.' The thought of all these poor people categorised by their particular brand of need, the endless research, the letters, the phone calls, the embarrassment of addressing so many strangers, all boggled my tired mind.

'No, Reinhardt, there must be a simpler way. In fact there is. Right here in our neighbourhood I'll bet you'd find at least one representative of each of the categories that you mention: one single parent, one sick person, one immigrant, one new arrival. They are all our neighbours and we have in common the fact that we all live on the same street. Why don't we concentrate on them? After all, Jesus told us to love our neighbours.'

'I don't think that's a very good idea,' countered Reinhardt. 'And anyway, how would we get started?'

'Well, why not invite them all to a special Christmas party next month?'

'Where?'

'Your house! It's nicer than mine.'

'Oh Justyn, I don't feel good about this idea.'

'Why not, Reinhardt?' I pushed him a little.

'Well, all right,' he conceded at last, 'but we won't ask the man who lives next door to me.'

'Whyever not?' I asked, surprised.

There was a pause. Eventually: 'We are not on speaking terms.'

'And why is that, may I be so bold as to ask?'

Again the pause. 'The fact of the matter is that he has this huge dog which comes through my fence and poops on my lawn. I have spent a fortune on the fence, but he still manages to get through. I have threatened to shoot the dog, and – well, we are not on speaking terms, me and my neighbour.'

So that was it. Reinhardt needed to invent a complicated approach to evangelising the whole town just so he could avoid loving his immediate neighbour! That's a long detour round a pile of poop!

I have to concede that it may on occasions be easier to share the gospel with strangers, but, even so, that very strangeness can make the message appear contrived, even phoney.

Driving through a small town recently, I noticed

on the reverse side of the 'Welcome to Hicksville'
sign the words: 'Leaving Hicksville city limits.
We're glad you came. Hurry back!' While I appreciate the sentiment, I question the sincerity. I hadn't
even stopped in Hicksville, let alone spent any
money. No one in that whole town knew my name.
No one knew what a very nice person I am – in fact
there wasn't a person in Hicksville who even knew
I existed on the face of the planet. How then could
they possibly be glad I came? And even if they did
know me, how in the world could the signwriter
(several years previously, from the appearance of
the peeling paint) have anticipated that my brief
visit to Hicksville would prove to be a happy one,
such as to inspire gladness in the good townsfolk of
that community? No! I had to come to the reluctant
conclusion that the sign was at best a cliché, and
probably a hypocritical waste of paint.

However, if the mayor of Hicksville had stepped
into the street and flagged me down and said, as
he handed me a glass of champagne: 'You're
Justyn Rees, the famous author of the book *Love
Your Neighbour for God's Sake* We are glad you
came to Hicksville. The town will never be the
same again. In fact, we're going to have a special
sign painted to commemorate this happy occasion.
Please hurry back!' Then the words would have
impressed me!

Just so, empty words like: 'I know that God has
brought you here to this place tonight so that you
can meet him personally,' when fired out from the
pulpit to fifteen hundred people, are relegated to
the same slot of the mind as Hicksville's 'We're

glad you came'. The preacher doesn't even know
I exist, let alone that I am here. How then could
he possibly know that God had brought me here so
he could meet me?

Such is the difficulty of evangelising strangers!

Who is my neighbour?

I'm glad that 'neighbour' is in the singular. 'Love
your neighbour' is so much more possible than
'Love all mankind'. Five billion people, is it?
I'll never get to meet most of them, let alone
love them!

So who is my neighbour? That question has a
familiar ring, like *déjà vu*. It was a lawyer who first
thought it up, as a cop-out. He was talking with Jesus
about what he would need to do to gain a ticket to
heaven. Jesus told him that if he was set on paying
his own fare then he would need to love God and
his neighbour perfectly. Taken aback by the sheer
impossibility of this, the lawyer tried to wriggle
out of the responsibility by pleading ignorance of
the precise identity of his neighbour. 'Who is my
neighbour?' he hedged.

So Jesus told him the now famous story of the
traveller who was misguided enough to travel from
Jerusalem to Jericho. The poor fellow was waylaid,
robbed and beaten to a pulp. The next two travellers
to pass that way were both religious, and therefore
well aware of their responsibility to love their
neighbour, yet failed to give the man so much
as a Kleenex. Finally along came the hero, the

Good Samaritan, who cleaned him up, took him to a motel and paid for his room in advance.

Now you might think that Jesus would bring out the moral of the story by repeating the lawyer's original question: 'Who is my neighbour?' But not so! Instead, he turned the question inside out: 'Whose neighbour are you?' – 'Which of these three do you think was a neighbour to the man who fell into the hands of robbers?' It would appear, therefore, that it is of greater importance that I prove to be a neighbour to whoever, than that I should do nothing while I procrastinate over who my neighbour actually is.

Meet Fred

So let me introduce you to Fred. I call him 'Fred' because 'neighbour' as in 'Love your neighbour' is too general a term, too theoretical a concept, to be a real, flesh-and-blood person. The point is that this book will be of limited use to you personally unless you come up with your own equivalent of 'Fred'. If, in the light of the chapters that follow, you are going to consider evangelism as anything other than something that other people ought to do to faceless strangers, then you must concentrate on a real flesh-and-blood person, someone you know personally, a neighbour, friend, fellow employee or student, even a relative. But get into your mind a name and face so that as I continue to refer to 'Fred' you can substitute your own friend's name and face.

Selah!

Fear of displaying ignorance

There is another big reason why some of us are embarrassed to share the gospel, even with people we know well. We are confused about the exact nature of the gospel and are afraid of displaying our ignorance. Consequently, when we get going we put the cart before the horse and confuse ourselves and Fred. We hesitate to say anything because we are unsure of all the facts.

'And how are you today?' asked a smoothly dressed man, in his grey striped suit and turquoise tie. The question of my well-being, on this day or any other, was in fact a matter of indifference to him, but convention required that the question be asked.

'Fine.' Convention was satisfied.

From vaulted ceiling to marble floor, the place spelled opulence. Gigantic potted shrubs sprouted across the picture windows that gave onto the street. Comfortable seats and soft nondescript music suggested that the possibility of being separated from more money than I could earn in a year was nothing to be afraid of!

'Is there anything I can help you with?'

'I'm in the market for a new car.'

'Well, you've come to the right place.' I suppose I could have made the error of looking in the chemist's . . .

'Did you have any particular model in mind?' I told him my preference.

At this delicate juncture in the negotiations he

could have made the same mistake that many
Christians make when trying to share their faith
with others. He could have taken me into one of
those little booths at the back of the showroom,
got out a contract and explained to me the steps
I could take to become the proud owner of one
of his magnificent automobiles. He could have
explained away the small print. He could have
let me read through the legal description of the
five-year warranty. He could have encouraged me
to count the cost, to recognise the sacrifice that I
would have to make; I would no longer be free
to consider other makes and models, but would
be committed to one car. Then there would be
the cost of insurance to take into consideration,
not to mention the cost of regular servicing and
maintenance. He could have reminded me of the
hours that would be required to wash and polish it at
weekends, the need to vacuum the carpets, to remove
the sticky sweets that would one day be dropped by
my kids between the cushions of the back seat. To
balance all that, he might have threatened me with
the alternatives: the horror of being the owner of a
Ford might well have motivated me to choose his
Honda . . .

But he didn't. In fact he said very little, beyond
'Let's take a look at one.' A peep at the engine
and a test drive later and I was his helpless victim.
I hardly noticed the small print. I suppose he did
explain the warranty, but I didn't hear. Yes, we
haggled over the price, but he knew he had me,
for he could see the glint in my eyes. I hardly
counted the zeros as I wrote the cheque, for the

sacrifice paled into insignificance by comparison with the gain.

Introducing Fred to Jesus is like that.

Of course it is helpful to explain the steps to be taken to become a Christian, but let him first experience Jesus before you confront him with a contract. Yes, of course there is more to it than asking Jesus into your heart, but must your friend examine all fifteen hundred pages of small print in both Hebrew and Greek before he can reach an intelligent decision? I know there are wonderful promises and assurances in the Bible, but Jesus himself is the focus. And I fully appreciate that there is a cost and a commitment involved, but if only Fred could first meet Jesus the sacrifice would cease to be one. The horror of the alternative to accepting Jesus might scare hell out of him, but the love of Jesus casts out fear and wins his heart.

Introduce Fred to Jesus, and let the question of how he becomes a Christian take care of itself later.

But what exactly is the gospel?

Relationship, not religion; introduction, not explanation

The gospel is not the steps to be taken to become a Christian; the gospel is Jesus.

The gospel is not a theological tome to be studied in multiple dead languages; it is the living, loving Son of God.

The gospel is not a deal to be negotiated with

God, a balance in which gain barely outweighs sacrifice, for God so loves that he freely gives Jesus.

The gospel is not a product, a religion which can be argued to be superior to its competitors. It is unique.

The gospel is not an eternal life policy to be sold to those afraid of hell. It is friendship with Jesus now and for ever.

The gospel is not about religion, but about relationship with God.

I once attended a conference of three or four hundred evangelists. 'What is the irreducible minimum of the gospel?' was one of the points we discussed. What are the bare facts that a man must know, that an evangelist must communicate, before genuine conversion can take place? The backdrop was painted as an evangelist waiting at a bus stop with a stranger. The time is very limited before the bus will come and the window of opportunity will be closed for ever. What must the poor, unsuspecting bus traveller know so that he can be saved before he finds escape in the arrival of the bus?

After hours of theological debate we boiled it all down to a few carefully worded sentences that contained the essential theological facts. It was a helpful exercise to ensure that what we were preaching was the truth, the whole truth and nothing but the truth, yet the stark statement that we distilled it all down to was as unpalatable as a vitamin tablet. The essential ingredients were present for eternal health and vitality, but no kind of hunger could ever be satisfied by swallowing that stuff. Doubtless the wretched man at the bus stop would have been driven to throw himself under the bus rather than swallow it.

The gospel is not a pill to be swallowed, to be washed down with soft music and sweet talk. Yes, there is a bare minimum to be communicated and believed, but you can express it in even less than a few sentences. In fact one word will suffice – 'Jesus'. The irreducible minimum of the gospel is the infinite eternal Jesus. To deny him is to be self-condemned. To acknowledge him is to be saved.

He is the way, for he it is who takes people all the way to God.

He is the truth. The essential facts and even the full unabridged fifteen-hundred-page version, small print and all, are in him. For he is the Word and all the promises of God find their 'yes' in him.

He is the life. To receive him is to receive eternal life. In him dwells all the fullness of God.

In short, the gospel is Jesus.

If the gospel was about *religion*, then evangelism could reasonably be described as an explanation of that religion. But as the gospel is about *relationship*, then evangelism is better described as an introduction. Explanations acquaint people with religious facts, but introductions lead people into relationship. To evangelise is therefore not so much an explanation of the steps to be taken to become a Christian. Rather, it is an introduction to Jesus Christ, who himself makes children of God out of ordinary people.

The original gospel

Preachers have a hard time when they seek a text of
Scripture which explains the ABC of how to become
a Christian. You would think, wouldn't you, that
Doctor Luke, when writing the book of Acts, would
have recorded at least one sermon from the lips of
Peter or Paul spelling out the transferable concepts
of how to become a Christian. And how is it that
the apostle Paul failed to include in all his prolific
correspondence a simple summary of the steps to
peace with God? Either the New Testament writers
have made a glaring oversight or else we are looking
for the wrong gospel.

So what is the right gospel? Simply Jesus. Did
Jesus commission his disciples to be witnesses of
how to become a Christian or to be witnesses
to him?

Suppose it had been possible to invite some of
the early evangelists to participate in the discussions
we held at that evangelists' conference I attended.
I wonder what they would have said about the
irreducible minimum of the gospel.

Chairman: Peter, you must have had a wonderful
    opportunity to preach the gospel that famous
    day of Pentecost, the morning when the Holy
    Spirit came on you all. We understand that a
    huge crowd of international tourists and pilgrims
    came running together to find out the cause of
    the commotion and that you addressed them.
    What was the bottom line of your message
    that day?

Peter: Well, the final punchline, which essentially summarised all I had been saying, was something along these lines: 'Therefore let all Israel be assured of this: God has made this Jesus, whom you crucified, both Lord and Christ.'

Chairman: But wasn't there some practical application given? Surely you must have told them what steps needed to be taken?

Peter: Yes, I did tell them to repent and be baptised, but not until they themselves had asked me what they needed to do.

Chairman: We have all read the account of the healing of the cripple at the Beautiful Gate of the Temple. I understand that the incident caused so much interest that the Temple authorities kept you in custody overnight. What did you tell them next morning when you were called to give an explanation? You did explain the gospel, didn't you?

Peter: I most certainly did. I would hardly miss an opportunity like that with all the leaders of my people being present. I told them: 'Know this, you and all the people of Israel: It is by the name of Jesus Christ of Nazareth, whom you crucified but whom God raised from the dead, that this man stands before you healed. Salvation is found in no one else, for there is no other name under heaven given to men by which we must be saved.'

Chairman: Why didn't you tell them how they could be saved?

Peter: How? The question was not of *how* they might be saved, but rather of *who* could save them! And I did make that very clear.

Chairman: From reading Doctor Luke's most precise account of your exploits, we understand that a few days later you, and all your colleagues this time, were put in jail and all made a miraculous escape. When the police caught up with you in the Temple next day, you must have been able to use the experience as a wonderful illustration of how people who pray the sinner's prayer can be set free from the bondage of sin. What did you tell them?

Peter: 'The God of our fathers raised Jesus from the dead – whom you had killed by hanging him on a tree. God exalted him to his own right hand as Prince and Saviour that he might give repentance and forgiveness of sins to Israel' – that's what I told them.

Chairman: You didn't lead them in the sinner's prayer?

Peter: I just told them about Jesus.

Chairman: So in each case you concentrated your message on Jesus himself rather than on how men should respond to him?

Peter: That is correct. I pointed them to Jesus and only when they asked how to respond did I tell them how to do so.

The next to contribute to the discussion would be Stephen. Doubtless he would be given an easy chair to compensate for the stoning he had suffered.

Chairman: Stephen, you must have preached a very eloquent sermon to elicit such a violent reaction. Most of us suffer from a non-reaction at the close of our sermons! You must have told those religious leaders that they all needed to become Christians. That would account for the outrage.

Stephen: Actually I gave a complete survey of the history of my people.

Chairman: But what of the practical application at the end?

Stephen: I told them that what they had done to Jesus was in the tradition of their fathers who had put to death the prophets who foretold Jesus' coming.

Chairman: Your angle, if I may call it that, was to use the Old Testament to point forward to Jesus. So, like the previous speaker, Jesus himself was your focus. Have I understood you correctly?

Stephen: That about sums it up.

Philip, described by Luke as 'the Evangelist', would have been right at home at an evangelists' conference.

Chairman: Philip, you are an evangelist of many years' experience. What was the irreducible minimum of your message during your famous Greater Samaria crusade?

Philip: I proclaimed to them the Christ.

Chairman: But what of your personal evangelism? When you were explaining things one to one, didn't you use a booklet or some kind of outline of the essential facts for salvation? What did you say to that Ethiopian, for example?

Philip: Well, when he picked me up as I was hitch-hiking along the road from Jerusalem to

Gaza, he was reading from chapter 53 of the book of Isaiah. Of course, it was a perfect set-up, so beginning with that Scripture I told him the good news of Jesus.

Chairman: So, whether in the pulpit or in personal conversation, you just told people about Jesus?

Philip: I did.

Paul, with his razor-sharp mind and his grasp of language, would have been a key contributor.

Chairman: Paul, your dramatic conversion on the Damascus road must have given you a wonderful testimony to recount. I believe you preached your first sermon as a Christian right there in Damascus. The facts of how you became a Christian must have been very fresh and undistorted. What did you tell them?

Paul: I just proclaimed Jesus, saying, 'He is the Son of God.'

Chairman: But surely as time went by you were forced to adopt a pattern of presentation, a simple outline of the ABC of becoming a Christian? After all, your conversion is held up by most preachers as the classic conversion of all time.

Paul: My message was essentially the same in all the many towns I visited. 'This Jesus, whom I proclaim to you, is the Christ.'

The conclusion seems inescapable. The early preachers of the gospel proclaimed Jesus himself, rather than the steps that should be taken to become a Christian.

Not 'how?' but 'who?'

It must be something to do with our inquisitive, do-it-yourself nature that promotes the question 'how?' over the question 'who?'. 'How does a man become a Christian?' is the question our gospel is always seeking to answer.

I daresay his friends called him 'Buff', but whatever his name the poor fellow had been blind since birth. It caused quite a stir, therefore, when Jesus spat on the ground, mixed the spittle with the dust and stuffed the resulting mud into Buff's useless eyes. Naturally he staggered over to the nearby pool of Siloam and swilled out the grit. Then, to his joy, he found he could see.

But seeing was one thing. Persuading others to believe that he really could see was quite another. For starters they wouldn't accept that this guy with 20/20 vision really was Buff. They even called his parents to identify him and to confirm that he had been born blind. And once Buff's identity had been established beyond reasonable doubt, the religious authorities hammered him with one recurring question: 'HOW?' How did he do it? How were your eyes opened? How could a man like Jesus do such a thing? When Buff failed to come up with a credible answer they threw him out of the Temple and shunned him.

For some reason no one had asked the most important question of all, at least not until Jesus found Buff after he had been excommunicated: 'Do you believe in the Son of Man?' Jesus asked.

'Who is he, sir, that I may believe in him?' The right question at last! – 'WHO?'

'I am.'

'Lord, I believe!' and he worshipped him.

I suppose subsequently he might have written (in Braille, of course) a tract entitled: 'How to receive your sight – three easy-to-follow steps'. It would have said:

Step 1 Mix a little spittle with some dust and make a paste.

Step 2 Rub paste thoroughly into eyes.

Step 3 Go and wash your eyes in water, preferably in the pool of Siloam.

I fear he would then have had many disappointed readers who, after endless experimentation with various brands of dust and temperatures of water, would have written the man off as a crank. For it is not *how* he was healed that was important, but rather *who* healed him. Just how Jesus did it is as much a mystery as how he saves sinners.

Why then do we concentrate our explanations of the gospel on answering the question: 'How do I become a Christian?' Jesus alone does it and Jesus alone knows how he does it. What we need to learn to do is to introduce people to Jesus and leave the saving up to him.

Simon, meet Jesus

Andrew wasn't put off evangelism by the fear of

talking to strangers. He just talked to his brother. Neither did he fear the embarrassment of not knowing all the facts. He just knew Jesus.

John the Baptist was a fiery evangelist who picked the hottest place on earth to hold his evangelistic meetings – the Jordan valley near the Dead Sea. I imagine him preaching from the middle of the river in his attempts to keep cool, up to his navel in water. Though he was foretelling the coming of Jesus rather than looking back on it, his message was much the same: 'After me will come one more powerful than I, the thongs of whose sandals I am not worthy to stoop down and untie. I baptise you with water, but he will baptise you with the Holy Spirit.'

The atmosphere must have been electric when one day he announced that the coming one was actually in the audience incognito. 'Among you stands one whom you do not know. He is the one I am talking about.' There must have been some old-fashioned sidelong glances. Anyone wearing shades would have been suspect.

But next day all was revealed. John was talking with two of his disciples. Suddenly he pointed to a lone figure walking along the river bank. 'There he is. The Lamb of God!'

'Let's follow him!' Andrew hissed to his companion. So off they went, keeping a discreet distance. Could this really be the long-awaited Messiah that they were following? What would he be like? Would he be real, in the sense that you could touch him, or would your hand go straight through? When he got round a corner would he just disappear, or would they see him levitate from the ground?

As they followed Jesus down the river bank, Andrew and his friend may have thought for a moment that they had lost him and ran to catch up. As the path went round a rock they came upon him suddenly, standing in the middle of the road, smiling at them.

'What are you looking for?'

'Who, us? Well . . .' What do you say when you run into the Son of God in the middle of the afternoon and he asks you what you've lost? 'Where are you staying?' It was a little lame, but it was the best they could come up with. To their amazement he invited them over for a coffee.

What they talked about as the sun set that evening is anyone's guess, so my guess is as good as anyone else's.

'Tell me about yourself, Andrew. What do you do for a living?'

'I am in the fishing industry. We have a small family business on the lake of Galilee.'

'And what of your family?'

'Well, my father's name is John. I have a brother named Simon. He's a bit of a lad, but I love him. We're in business together.'

'I'd like to meet him, you know. Could you arrange it, Andrew?'

'Just name the time and place and I'll get him there.'

What excitement Andrew and his friend must have felt as they hurried home later that evening. 'I can't wait to tell Simon about this!' So he didn't. As soon as he got back to the place where they were staying, Andrew found Simon. 'Hey,

Simon, you'll never guess who we just had supper with!'

'Pontius Pilate?'

'No. It was the one Moses and the prophets wrote about. The Messiah!'

'Go on! You're kidding me. You just sat down to tea with the Messiah? Who else was there, the Pope and the President of the United States? Get real, Andrew!'

'No. Straight up. It really was the Messiah and his name is Jesus. He lives in Nazareth.'

'Did he have a halo, or perhaps wings bulging from under his shirt? Did he glow in the dark?'

'I don't care what you say, it's still true. And anyway he wants to meet you, so I set up an appointment at the restaurant on the corner of King's Road for tomorrow at 10.30. I hope you're free?'

I really don't know how cynical Simon was. How would I feel if my brother came and told me he'd just had tea with God? How would Fred feel?

Next morning at 10.29 Andrew and Simon enter the restaurant. There is Jesus in a booth. The conversation must have gone something like this.

'Good morning, Jesus. This is my brother Simon, the one I was telling you about. Simon, this is the Messiah, Jesus.'

At this point Andrew's job was done. He had brought together two people he loved and introduced them by name to each other. Now all he needed to do was to stand by and see what happened.

'So you're Simon Johnson!' says Jesus, reaching out and grabbing him by the hand. 'I'm going to call you Peter – Rocky!'

Was that effective evangelism? Did Andrew communicate to his brother the essential facts for salvation? How well versed in Christian apologetics was Andrew and how did he fare in the face of his brother's scepticism? Did he lead him in the sinner's prayer? I don't know, but one way or the other Peter was hooked, to use a good fishing expression.

Basic introductions

So this book is about introducing a real neighbour, whom we will call Fred, to Jesus.

The story goes of a British ship which sank somewhere in the south Pacific. Many were drowned, but two Welshmen swam to a nearby island. When they had got their breath back, they started a choir. Amazingly, two Scots made it to another of the islands with which the ocean was dotted. They emptied their pockets and started a bank. Two Irish reached yet a third island, and immediately started a fight. So it may not altogether surprise you to learn that two Englishmen escaped death by swimming to a fourth island. But when they got there, they did nothing. After all, they had not been officially introduced!

It would be a tragedy if Fred and Jesus were to do nothing together through lack of a simple introduction. And introductions are simple. They contain little more than the people's names and a bare minimum of basic information.

'Fred, this is Jesus, the Son of God. Jesus, this is Fred, my next-door neighbour.'

If your introduction is successful it may lead to physical contact like a handshake, accompanied by an exchange of 'How do you do's. But be aware that simple introductions can lead to commitments that last a lifetime.

2

Too Shy to be Introduced

Understanding prejudice against meeting invisible strangers

If it's tough to make a simple introduction between Jesus and Fred, both of whom you know and love, how much more difficult is it for Fred to accept the introduction! Fred may know and love you, but Jesus is a whole different ball game. He's an invisible, inaudible stranger.

There are huge barriers that Fred will have to overcome if he's to start to develop any kind of relationship with Jesus. But Jesus is very skilled at dealing with such difficulties and specialises in breaking down every dividing wall of hostility.

Yet it may be a good idea to take an honest look at the difficulties early on in this book, not to dampen our ardour but rather to make us more sympathetic to Fred's problems.

Fred can't see Jesus' face

The telephone is an invention that I abhor. It always rings when I am sitting down to a meal with my family. It always takes precedence over 'live' people, so if I am standing in line at an information desk and the phone rings, it jumps the queue every time. Most of all I dislike the instrument because I cannot see the person I am talking to. Body language plays a large part in every conversation but bodies don't communicate well over the phone. I hardly ever used the phone until I was through my teens, and on the occasions I could not escape its use I would get all tongue-tied and self-conscious. Silly, really, but just how is Fred supposed to feel when I ask him to talk to a God whose face and body language he cannot see?

The young teens group from our church were having what they termed 'a spy hunt' in the local shopping centre. Some of us parents were conscripted by the youth leader to be spies – in disguise, as the kids knew us well. The object of the game was for the young people to identify the spies; when a suspect was spotted they were to be challenged with the words: 'Mummy, Mummy, Daddy, Daddy'.

Each of us arrived at the shopping mall complete with camouflage. One couple had blackened their skin with boot polish and had scrounged strange clothes from the church's lost-property box. Another had a cowboy outfit, and so on. I resolved to go as the invisible man. I wrapped bandages around my head, leaving just a slit for the eyes which I obscured with dark glasses. I wore a hat on my head and a light-coloured raincoat. My hands I stuffed in my pockets. The effect was impressive, judging from the strange looks I received as I walked about. A security guard eyed me suspiciously and followed me into the Gents where I went to adjust the bandages, which were slipping. He watched silently in the mirror as I unwrapped the bandages, and when a relatively normal face appeared he asked me what I thought I was playing at. My explanation that I was a spy and must not be recognised did little to calm his fears, so I confessed all and he was satisfied.

With my disguise back in place I went and sat on a bench near the waterfall in the main concourse. I could see the young people as they came and went. They knew perfectly well that no normal person would sit around the mall looking the way I did so I must be part of the game, yet none of them dared approach me. They passed by several times, eyeing me self-consciously. At first I wondered what was wrong, then it occurred to me that they were afraid to address someone whose face they could not see.

God has said that 'no man can see my face and live'. Very graciously, therefore, he has hidden his face from us. But until you grow accustomed to prayer, it is hard to speak to someone whose face you cannot see. And it's hard for Fred to be introduced to one who is invisible.

Fred can't hear Jesus' voice

An ancient aunt once phoned me. She loved to talk
on the phone and I knew I was in for a long session.
In the middle of the conversation there was a click
and a crackle as someone in another part of the house
lifted a receiver. I was cut off. There was nothing
I could do so I hung up, secretly relieved. Ten
minutes later I lifted the receiver with the intention
of making another call. Instead of the dialling tone,
I heard a familiar voice chattering away – my dear
aunt, oblivious to my absence, had just kept right
on talking!

But for most of us it is hard to carry on a
one-sided conversation. Even the occasional 'Uhuh'
or 'Yes' or 'You don't say!' helps the conversation
on no end.

I used to fly as a commercial pilot. Flying a
small four-seater Piper into a busy airfield, I was
embarrassed to discover that my radio was on the
blink. I made the usual call: 'White Planes, this is
Piper Cherokee 333P on a five-mile final for 24.'
No response. I tried again. 'White Planes, this is
Piper Cherokee 333P on a four-mile final for 24.'
Still no response. I was conscious of the unease
of my three passengers. It occurred to me that,
just maybe, I was transmitting while my receiver
was inoperative. Perhaps the controller in the tower
could hear me while I could not hear him. So I tried
again: 'White Planes, this is Piper Cherokee 333P
on a three-mile final for 24. Am experiencing radio
difficulties. If I am clear to land please show me
a green light.' I suddenly felt very self-conscious,

knowing that the passengers were listening to
what was probably me talking to myself. No one
on the ground was listening: I was just saying
words into a plastic microphone. But a moment
later I got my green light from the tower and
I knew my message had been heard. I had no
audible reply, but I could see the response to my
request.

It takes a while to get the hang of praying with
no audible response. However, a few green lights
and definite responses to my requests and I get the
impression that someone is listening. But for Fred,
who has never prayed, that is a difficult hurdle
to jump.

I was speaking to a young people's group on the
subject of prayer. They were a conglomeration of
youth groups from both sides of the US/Canadian
border. Before the session started I found an unused
Sunday School room in the church basement and
concealed in it a wireless microphone, which I
wrapped up in a collapsed umbrella and left on a
desk. As I got going on my topic I told them how
hard it is to speak to God when you can't hear his
replies.

'OK, I want a volunteer,' I demanded. 'Someone
who will make a statement justifying American
independence from British rule.' That got a response
from a young lady with five pins in each ear
and a studded leather jacket with a large Stars
and Stripes on the back. I left the main group
to talk quietly among themselves and took the
girl down to the basement and into the room
where I had hidden the microphone. 'Now,' I

said, 'why don't you make your statement? Put as much feeling as you can into it and address the umbrella.' She did a fair job, but her heart wasn't in it, for she thought no one was listening. When she had finished what she understood to be the dummy run she asked eagerly: 'Can we go and say it now?' 'No,' says I. 'You don't need to say it twice.'

'But I was only practising.'

'No, you just said it to the whole group.'

'I didn't! There's only you listening.'

'Not so, I assure you. There are over a hundred other people listening to every word we say.'

'Never!'

Nothing would convince her in that quiet room that she had a vast audience of very amused teenagers. It wasn't until we walked back into the sanctuary amid hoots of laughter and applause that she believed me.

Little wonder, then, that it is hard for Fred, unfamiliar as he is with prayer, to grasp the truth that as he opens his mouth to pray in the secret of his own room, he has an audience with the King of kings.

Fred can't shake Jesus' hand

Some people are huggers. Some are kissers. Some rub noses. But most of us are shakers, hand shakers. 'How do you do? I'm pleased to meet you,' you recite as you grasp hands and pump them up and down in synchronisation.

Some handshakes give you the sensation of grasping an under-cooked fillet of sole. Others grind your knuckles to splinters before you have a chance to get a decent grip. But one way or another, personal contact is made.

Imagine being introduced to a person. You make the expected noises about being pleased to make their acquaintance. Then you reach out your hand, only to find the poor thing abandoned there, hanging limply in the breeze, groping lamely for a response. If words are not followed up by touch, the introduction may well be still-born.

Touch is a vital element of interaction. Without it you remain isolated and apart. I am told that a baby will gain no weight, no matter how much nourishment is plugged into its mouth, if it is deprived of the warmth of human touch.

I went to see an old lady in the hospital the other day. She was nearing the end of a long struggle with cancer.

'Is there anything I can do to help?' I asked.

'Just hold my hand,' she replied.

Personal touch is so reassuring, but no help to Fred. It's hard to meet someone whose hand he cannot feel, let alone shake.

Fred is unsure how to address Jesus

Names are a wonderful bridge. If you can remember a person's name, they feel so special. Forget it, and they are insulted.

In my job I move around a fair bit and meet

many groups of people. It kills me when I cannot remember someone. The most difficult is when I know the person quite well but for some reason his name has just gone. Far from being a bridge, his name, or perhaps the lack of it, is a positive barrier to communication, and I studiously avoid encountering him until I have pulled up the correct mental file. Sometimes I stall for a while in the hope that it will return, but I frequently get caught. The other day I was speaking at a camp. 'Do you remember me from last year?' inquired a bright young face.

'Yes,' I said, relieved that I really did remember. 'You're Vanessa.'

She glowed.

Next to her was another eager face. 'Do you remember me from last year?'

Well, in all honesty I didn't, but I couldn't bear to insult her.

'I remember your face, but your name has gone.' (God be merciful to me, a sinner.)

'No wonder you don't remember my name. I wasn't here last year. We've never met before!' Served me right!

But in addition to knowing a person's name, you also need to know the correct form of address. Lots of people have an awareness of a 'higher power'. But addressing that higher power can be difficult. 'Oh, Higher Power, I'm Fred. Pleased to meet you. Can I call you HP?'

I remember doing a two-minute 'pause for thought' on BBC Radio 2. The phone rang while I was still in the studio and a very cultured voice said: 'I'm Lady Salisbury. Very impressed with what you just said. I'd like to meet you some time.' I was duly grateful for the encouragement and asked where we might meet. 'How about my place?' she suggested.

I asked what I took to be a very reasonable question. 'Where do you live?'

'Hatfield House,' was the stark reply. Well I'd never been to Hatfield so I made the mistake of asking for an address. 'Just follow the main road. You'll see it.'

So when I arrived in Hatfield, in good time for the appointment, I discovered to my dismay that Hatfield House was rather like Buckingham Palace and occupied half of Hatfield.

I was challenged at the gate by a policeman. 'Justyn Rees to see Lady Salisbury.'

'Yes, sir. You are expected,' and he directed me to a door at the back of the house. I have never seen so grand a front door as this imposing back entrance. I parked my shabby little car and bravely rang the bell. A real butler opened the door and showed me into a vast room furnished with priceless antiques. A fire blazed in the old-fashioned hearth. 'Her ladyship will be with you shortly,' he announced and left me.

Suddenly something near panic gripped me. How should I address the lady? 'Your ladyship? . . . My lady? . . . Lady Salisbury? . . . Lady? . . . Mrs Salisbury?' I didn't know. There weren't any Ladies on my side of the tracks. The whole meeting was spoiled for me by my discomfort over simple ignorance of the proper etiquette.

No wonder it is hard for Fred to address God for the first time. Perhaps that is why the very first thing Jesus taught his disciples when introducing them to his Father was the correct manner of addressing him. 'When you pray, say: "Our Father . . ."'

Fred may feel alienated from Jesus

'God would never be interested in meeting me,' declared a girl in her late teens. We were holding an open discussion in a restaurant called The Hungry Hippo. The subject was 'Meeting God' and I had delivered invitation cards all over town which had attracted lots of people I had never met.

'If you knew the things I have done!' she continued. 'I have broken every rule in the book. I would feel most uncomfortable if God walked into this room.'

From the other side of the room came a response. 'Six months ago, if someone had told me that I would be party to a discussion like this I would have laughed in their face. I was on the street making a living out of men's weakness. A stranger came up to me and told me God loved me. I told him to get lost, but he said he'd pray for me. I told him God could never love me. He said something about God loving unconditionally. I didn't understand what he meant, but I do now. I know that God loves me despite all I have done.'

Perhaps Fred might also feel embarrassed to shake hands with one so holy as Jesus.

Fred may bear a grudge against Jesus

'We don't talk about God in this house,' said an affronted lady whose door I had knocked on as part of a neighbourhood visitation programme.

'Oh,' I said, 'and why is that?'

'If you must know, my son fell ill. We prayed that God would make him better, but he died. I see no reason why I should speak to a God who so badly fails people who look to him for help in time of need!'

'How long ago was that?' I enquired gently.

'Must be over twenty years now.'

For two decades that woman had been unwilling to meet Jesus because she was so angry with him. If someone had told her that she was a sinner and needed to repent before God, she would have punched them. From her perspective it was God who needed to repent, not her. She was the injured party.

Another man I met wanted nothing to do with God. When I pressed him for the reason he told me that, when he was a child, he and his kid brother had climbed up on to the barn roof. 'I can fly and Jesus will catch me,' the little boy had chanted as he jumped. Jesus didn't catch him.

Perhaps Fred is also angry with Jesus over what he sees to be his culpable negligence.

Fred may not be impressed by the crowd Jesus hangs out with

Bill was a neighbour and a friend. He didn't share my faith, but we got on well. I heard that an evangelist was coming to town, setting up his tent and holding a crusade. Bill asked me what it was all about. 'I don't know the preacher, but we could go along and have a listen, if you like.' I couldn't believe my luck when Bill agreed to come.

We approached the tent along with streams of enthusiastic saints, all eager for the best seats. Bill and I sat near the back. The singing was full of gusto, but if you didn't know the tune you felt like an outsider. The prayers were long and fervent, but Bill took the opportunity for a snooze. The appeal for funds which culminated in the offering brought tears to the eyes and cash to the plate. But it was the sermon which finished us. After enduring twenty minutes of shouting, finger-pointing and tear-jerking illustrations, Bill turned and whispered to me: 'Would you buy a used car from that man?' I shook my head. 'Then why the hell are we wasting our time sitting here!' We left.

Those who promote the sales of motor cars know full well that the customer, who probably knows little or nothing about the finer points of engineering and design, will base his decision on his confidence in the salesperson. That's why they spend millions on TV commercials promoting, not their latest models, but their salespeople.

I fear that one of the greatest barriers to the gospel is the people who preach it. People just cannot take evangelists. Perhaps Fred has been watching too much television to be impressed with the Jesus crowd.

Fred may be scared off by the fear of a big commitment

You are being set up on a blind date. You have never met the person before, but your friend assures you that you'll just love him (or her, depending upon your taste!). 'He's everything you ever hoped for in a man. Before the evening is over you'll be madly in love.' You are a little sceptical, but hey! Sounds like a fun evening. But then your friend continues: 'There is one thing I should make clear from the outset. This guy really means business. Over dinner he will ask you to marry him and you must say "Yes!" He will without a doubt make you the happiest wife in all the world. Of course, if you should be foolish enough to turn him down, you have no alternative but to face a life of regrets as an old maid who let her chance pass her by. He may never ask you again and there is no other for you.'

Placing such a heavy agenda on a simple introduction would probably ruin the anticipation of what might otherwise prove a happy evening!

So why should it be different for Fred when we are setting him up on a blind date with God, whom he hardly knows? 'I want to take you to a meeting where a man will tell you all about God. At the end he will ask you to commit your whole life to God, and you must accept. This decision will prove to be the great turning point of your whole life, the gateway to heaven itself. But should you fail to accept, then you will have to face up to the possibility of an eternity of regrets.'

Most sensible people spend months or years getting to know each other before even broaching the subject of a life-long commitment. Why must we, therefore, feel obligated to dump an eternal commitment on poor Fred the very first time we make an introduction?

'Oh, but we must preach the whole counsel of God. What if this were Fred's last chance? It is written "Today is the day of salvation".'

If we don't trust in the patience and grace of the God to whom we are seeking to introduce Fred, then I doubt Fred will ever be inclined to so trust, either!

Fred has no faith in Jesus

There are many barriers that make the introduction of Fred to Jesus difficult, but they all boil down to a matter of faith. You relate to Fred by sight, and have learned to trust him. But you relate to Jesus by faith alone. You have grown used to relating to him by faith and accept it as a perfectly normal and valid state of affairs. But this is all new to Fred.

The Bible says: 'The god of this age has blinded the minds of unbelievers, so that they cannot see the light of the gospel of the glory of Christ, who is the image of God.' Whatever guises the barriers may come in, the underlying reason is spiritual blindness which denies faith.

How then shall I introduce Fred to Jesus?

3

Introductions are Made by Name

Fred, this is Jesus.
Jesus, this is Fred

How shall I introduce Fred to Jesus? How do you make any introduction? By name, of course.

For us mortals a name is a label, a tag, a sound, the resonance of which in the eardrums will recall to the front of the brain the associated face and attributes of the person to whom that name belongs.

I was speaking at a men's conference in Florida. The invitation did wonders for my ego. I would be able to add to my CV: 'International conference speaker who travels from coast to coast preaching the Word!' But when I arrived I felt terribly far from home and wondered why it had been necessary for me to fly all the way from the west coast of Canada to the south-east United States. Surely there would be someone nearer who could have done the speaking?

I checked in at the registration desk and was given the usual pack of conference materials, lay-out of the conference centre, timetable, name label, etc. I dutifully pinned on the tag: 'Justyn Rees, Plenary Speaker'. That helped. Then I went and found my room. As I unpacked, I discovered that I had neglected to pack my toothpaste. It would never do for an international plenary speaker to have bad breath, so I jumped in my rented car and drove to a nearby shopping centre.

As I was paying for my tube of Crest, the girl at the till said: 'That will be $3.45, Mr Rees.' I was famous! Even the girl at the drug store knew my name! Perhaps I was internationally known, after all.

'That's very impressive,' I glowed. 'How do you know my name?'

'Not difficult. It's printed in big letters on the label pinned to your chest!'

Names are a vital part of establishing a link between two people. They form the initial bridge over which further interaction can follow. My problem is remembering the person's name. I think it must be part of my shyness. So up-tight and self-conscious am I when meeting new people that I frequently fail to listen to what is being said. 'Justyn, this is my friend Richard.' I echo the sound: 'Hi, Richard. Good to meet you,' but the name never gets past my random access memory to my hard drive. Having repeated the sound, I lose it, and ten seconds later I couldn't tell you the name for love nor money.

I once saw a book advertised, entitled *How to Stop*

Forgetting. I sent away for a copy. It duly arrived with the invoice enclosed. It took two reminders before I remembered to pay!

The book taught various methods of remembering people's names. Rhyming ideas was one: it worked by imagining the person in the rhyming circumstance. 'Fred' you visualised in 'bed'. 'Jane' writhing in 'pain', 'Russ' travelling in a 'bus', and so on. Alternatively, it suggested that you could associate the new face with someone you already know who has the same name. Yet another method is to associate a person's name with an object, so I could have remembered 'Richard' by thinking of lots of money, or 'Rosemary' with a flower, 'Rob' with a thief and 'Sandy' with a beach. I have seldom found this method to fail.

But when it does fail the results can be embarrassing. I recall a friend of mine who was chairman of our church council. A very irate neighbour came storming into our meeting one day. After introducing herself as 'Mrs Bosomworth', she went into a long tirade which culminated with a threat to sue the church if the matter was not rectified. My friend the chairman very graciously thanked her for drawing the matter to our attention, '. . . and we do hope that this will not stand in the way of our being good neighbours, Mrs Bottomly'. The lady sued!

God's name is more than a label

Names are more important than just labels when it comes to introducing people to God. For one thing,

you can't see God and his name is all we have to
go on. I say 'All we have to go on' tongue in cheek,
because, with God, his name is far more than a sound
that recalls his attributes. Let me explain what I have
in mind.

Moses, who had been brought up in the palace
of Pharaoh in Egypt, decided at the age of forty to
do what he could to improve the pitiful lot of his
own ethnic people, the Hebrews, who were currently
slaves to the Egyptians. His efforts amounted to
little more than the murder of one Egyptian who
had been abusing a Hebrew. But that was enough
to turn Moses from prince to fugitive, and he fled to
the wilderness to the east of Egypt. There he spent
the next forty years of his life scratching a living as
a shepherd.

One day, when Moses was eighty years old, he
noticed a bush with flames coming from it, which
apparently was not being consumed. 'Hello, what's
this?' he thought to himself as he walked over to get
a closer look.

God spoke: 'Moses, take your shoes off, for you're
walking on holy ground.' God went on to tell him to
go back to Egypt and to take the lead in liberating
the Hebrew slaves.

'Tell me,' said Moses, 'when someone asks:
"What is the name of the God who sent you
to do this?", what shall I say?' (How am I to
introduce you?)

'I am who I am,' was God's reply.

That was not just a label, a tag by which the
attributes of the God of the Hebrews could be dif-
ferentiated from those of the gods of the Egyptians.

Neither was it a very handy name for introductions. No, it seems that God was saying something along these lines: 'My name is who I am. Express my name and you express me.'

Let me build a little more on that thought.

Some time later, after Moses had succeeded in leading the Hebrews out of Egypt, he brought them back to the territory with which he was most familiar, the wilderness where he had spent the past forty years. There God gave him the Ten Commandments. One day Moses asked God a favour. The conversation went something like this . . .

Moses: You have given me the very important task of leading this people. You have said that I have found favour in your sight. You seem to know me by my name – Moses. But I want to ask you to give me a very special assurance of your presence with me. How do I know you are really there?

God: My presence will go with you and I will give you rest.

Moses: Well, thanks for saying that, but would I be asking too much if I asked to see you?

God: I will indeed make you aware of the reality of my presence, but not visually, for if you were to see my face you would die. I will convince you of the reality of my presence audibly. I will proclaim before you my name.

God appointed a rendezvous up Mount Sinai, at the mouth of a cave. Early next morning Moses was there, rather nervously clutching two more blank sheets of rock. He had dropped the first two on which God had written the Commandments and needed a replacement copy.

At the appointed hour God descended in a cloud. Moses saw nothing, for the hand of God was over his eyes and he was lost in a swirling mist. But he heard plenty, and what he heard did more to convince him of the reality of God's presence than the evidence of his eyes could ever have achieved. He heard the Lord's name proclaimed and it sounded like this:

> The Lord, the Lord, the compassionate and gracious God, slow to anger, abounding in love and faithfulness, maintaining love to thousands, and forgiving wickedness, rebellion and sin. Yet he does not leave the guilty unpunished; he punishes the children and their children for the sin of the fathers to the third and fourth generation.

Moses fell flat on his face in worship because of the overwhelming reality of the presence of God which accompanied the proclamation of his name.

Now that is just what we want as we introduce Fred to Jesus: an overwhelming sense of the presence of God such that he will fall down in worship.

In the New Testament we read that Peter, James and John had a very similar experience to that of Moses. They were hiking up a mountain with Jesus, much as Moses had been. Suddenly, to their great amazement, the face of Jesus started to shine with the glory of God. Two other men, Elijah and Moses, came from nowhere and talked with Jesus. Peter babbled some incoherent nonsense about building three booths. Then the hand of God was over their eyes, just as it had been over Moses' eyes, and a bright cloud swirled across their vision. They saw nothing, but what they heard convinced them beyond any shadow of doubt of the presence of God. 'This is my beloved Son with whom I am well pleased. Listen to him.'

The three disciples fell on their faces in awe, just as Moses had done. God had bestowed on his Son the name above every name, that at the name of Jesus every knee should bow and every tongue confess his Lordship.

After Jesus had ascended to heaven, having been crucified, buried and raised again, the disciples were still faced with a world full of needy people. They had grown accustomed to bringing people to Jesus personally and saying: 'Jesus, this is Elizabeth. She has terrible arthritis. Would you please touch her and make her well?' 'This is Kevin. He's deaf. Would you pop your fingers in his ears and let him hear?' But now that the visible presence of Jesus was removed from the scene, what were they to do?

The first need to present itself was that of a life-long cripple who used to sit begging at the Beautiful Gate of the Temple. As Peter and John were passing one afternoon, he requested financial help. Being penniless, they declined to oblige. If only Jesus was walking with them, he wouldn't just toss a penny into the man's hat. He would heal him.

But Jesus had left them a promise – in fact several promises.

One of them was: 'Where two or three come together in my name, there am I with them.' There were two of them, Peter and John. That constituted a quorum. Jesus must be there somewhere.

Another promise was: 'I will do whatever you ask in my name, so that the Son may bring glory to the Father.'

So Peter, who had been introduced by his brother Andrew to Jesus three years previously, now passed on the introduction, introducing the cripple to Jesus by name: 'In the name of Jesus Christ of Nazareth, walk.' The cripple saw nothing, not even a swirling cloud or the hand of God. But what he heard convinced him beyond any shadow of doubt that God was present. He heard proclaimed the name above every name, the name to which every knee shall bow and the name that every tongue will some day confess as Lord – Jesus.

He didn't fall on his face in worship, as Moses and Peter had done. First he stood, then he walked, then he ran, then he leaped. Finally, with his whole being he praised the God who was present.

That is what we want our friends to do as we introduce them to Jesus.

In the name of Jesus

So the name of Jesus is a vital part of our introduction between him and Fred. The presence of Fred is undeniable, for he is visible, tangible and audible, possibly even smellable. But the presence of Jesus is rendered undeniable by the proclamation of his name, the I AM – JESUS.

Here, then, is where we are going with this thought in the remainder of this book:

- we must show kindness in his name, for he has promised that 'Anyone who gives a cup of water in my name will certainly not lose his reward';
- we must meet in his name, for he has promised that 'Where two or three come together in my name, there am I with them';
- we must welcome others in his name, for he has promised that 'Whoever welcomes one of these little children in my name welcomes me';
- we must pray in his name, for he has promised that 'I will do whatever you ask in my name';
- we must worship his name, for he promises to 'inhabit the praises of his people', those who praise his name;
- we must be united in his name, for he taught that unity would be the hallmark to let the world know that God loves them;
- we must talk in his name, for we are told that 'Faith comes from . . . the preaching of Christ' (the proclaiming of his name);
- we must help our friends to be reconciled in his name, for he promised that all who repent in his name will receive the forgiveness of their sins;

- we must help our friends to believe in his name, for we are promised that 'To all . . . who believe in his name, he gives the right to become children of God';
- we must help our friends confess his name, for we are promised that 'Everyone who calls on the name of the Lord will be saved';
- we must encourage our friends to be baptised in his name, for we are commanded to 'Go and make disciples of all nations, baptising them in the name of the Father and of the Son and of the Holy Spirit'.

Yes, introductions need to be made by name.

But first things first. The initial objective of any introduction is to get the two parties talking. Start the dialogue and you are 90 per cent of the way there.

4

Just Get Them Talking

Speaking with someone is a thousand times better than just speaking about them

Sarah owned and operated the Rising Sun, a pub three miles from our former home in Kent. Over the bar one day we got talking about famous people we had met. She dropped a few names, of which my wife Joy and I had never heard. We were not impressed, and she was unimpressed with our ignorance of people that mattered.

'Well, I know Billy Graham,' I countered.

'Yes, but does he know you?'

I had to admit that I had merely shaken hands with him on one brief occasion, so my attempt at name-dropping was quickly called. Then a new thought: 'But I do know Cliff Richard, and what's more he knows me. Beat that!'

Sarah was impressed, but wanted details. 'I actually sang with him on stage on one occasion.' (It had been a relatively small gathering and the stage was but six feet square, but I neglected to share those details.) Sarah, being a teen of the sixties, was a great fan of Cliff Richard, so her eyes grew round. She wanted to know all I could tell her about him, every little detail.

'I can do better than that,' I boasted. 'I could introduce you to him.'

It so happened that Billy Graham was visiting London for a pre-crusade meeting in the Royal Albert Hall and Cliff Richard was to be the featured singer. Instantly forgetting her religious scruples, Sarah agreed to come.

We sat way up in the gallery. Even through binoculars Cliff looked very small. 'Some introduction,' sneered Sarah.

When the programme was nearly over we crept out. 'Where are we going?' Sarah protested.

'To meet Cliff Richard.'

We must have climbed down hundreds of steps and walked round miles of curving passages, but eventually we came to a door which said: 'Stage door. No admittance'. It was unlocked, so we went in. And there he was, the man himself – Cliff Richard.

'Hello, Justyn,' he said. 'And what are you doing here?'

'I want you to meet our friend. Cliff, this is Sarah. Sarah, this is Cliff Richard.' Oh, what a victory! But there was more to come. While we were talking Billy Graham came into the room. Seeing strangers there, he gave us a half smile.

'Dr Graham,' said Cliff. 'This is Justyn Rees, his wife Joy and their friend Sarah.'

'Justyn Rees,' repeated Billy thoughtfully. 'I knew your father. Didn't we meet once before?'

Game, set and match!

The point is that far better than merely talking *about* a person is the joy of talking *to* the person. And far better than telling a friend *about* Jesus is the joy of getting them talking *to* Jesus.

So how can we get Fred into conversation with Jesus?

Fred and Jesus over coffee

Imagine yourself sitting at your kitchen table. At each end of the table sits a friend of yours and you are in the middle. So there are three of you. You are on intimate terms with the other two, but they are complete strangers to each other. There is no communication between them, first because they are strangers, but more immediately because one doesn't even know the other is there. Are you getting the picture? On your left hand is your good friend, Fred. And on your right hand is Jesus. The circumstances demand that you make the introduction. Your job is to get them talking. It's not your responsibility to edge the conversation round to topics like eternal destiny, or even confessions of sin or statements of faith. Just get them talking. An exchange of names is a start. The weather is tried and tested. Last night's football game is often a good ice-breaker. Just get them started.

So how? I suggest you turn and address your friend on the right – Jesus. In fact, to make it easier, imagine that Fred is no longer in the room, for his presence might make you feel awkward as you talk to Jesus about him.

Talk with Jesus about Fred

It would be going too far to make a general principle out of it, but it is my observation that very rarely do people become Christians unless someone, somewhere, has been praying for them by name.

On countless occasions I have asked groups of Christians to put their hands up if, to the best of their knowledge, no one prayed for them by name prior to their becoming a Christian. I recall an occasion when one girl put up her hand. Her friend sitting next to her said acidly: 'Put your hand down, you fool. I was praying for you!'

Faith is a vital ingredient and without faith it is impossible to please God, but Fred has no faith. Fred doesn't believe that Jesus is God, or that he shed his blood on the cross for Fred's forgiveness, or that he rose again, or that his Holy Spirit can indwell Fred, making all the promises of God germinate into life. Fred doesn't, but you do. So believe for him. Make a daily habit of stating your faith in these facts on behalf of Fred: 'Father, I believe that Jesus died and shed his precious blood for my friend Fred. I believe he rose again so that Fred can have eternal life. I believe that the Holy Spirit can live in Fred's heart and that all your promises hold true for Fred as they do for me. And I ask in Jesus' name that Fred may come to believe as I do.'

*   *   *

Arnold Fruchtenbaum is Jewish. He was born and brought up in Germany and his family endured terrible hardship through the Second World War, but they survived. In the years after the war ended he and his family were housed in a series of refugee camps, and it was in one of these that a Lutheran pastor, Theo Burgstahler, and his daughter Hannah visited the Fruchtenbaum family. Though the visit made little impression on Arnold, who was still a young boy, God impressed Arnold and his family on the heart of Hannah. She resolved to pray for each member of the family by name.

Soon after, in 1949, the Fruchtenbaum family received visas for the United States and Hannah lost touch with them. Nevertheless she prayed on, naming them almost daily before her heavenly Father. Eight years later, shortly before her father's death, Hannah asked him: 'Father, shall I continue to pray for the Fruchtenbaums?'

'Yes, my dear. One day you will know that your prayers have been answered.'

That very year, in far-off Brooklyn, New York, Arnold Fruchtenbaum was introduced to Jesus and became a radiant Christian. He didn't know that anyone had prayed for him. Not only did he become a Christian, he founded an organisation dedicated to introducing fellow Jews to Jesus. He wrote books.

In 1984 Hannah Burgstahler, now an elderly lady, received an interesting gift from her husband. 'I was in the Christian bookshop and bought this book on prophecy that I thought might interest you.' He passed her a book entitled *In the Footsteps of the Messiah*, but it wasn't the title that caught her eye so much as the name of the author. 'Arnold Fruchtenbaum,' she read. 'How strange. That is a name I have laid before God constantly these past thirty-five years. Could it be the same Arnold Fruchtenbaum that I visited all those years ago?'

So she wrote to the publisher and asked if the author had a father and mother, brothers and sisters named . . . (She knew the names so well, for she had recited them before her heavenly Father for so many years.) If so, she would appreciate an address where she could contact him.

Imagine Arnold's joy at receiving a letter from a distant benefactor who had believed on his behalf all those years and he had never known about it.

No, I wouldn't go so far as to say that no one becomes a Christian unless they are prayed for by name, but I would underscore the promise of Jesus: 'I will do whatever you ask in my name, so that the Son may bring glory to the Father . . . You may ask me for anything in my name, and I will do it. I tell you the truth, my Father will give you whatever you ask in my name. Until now you have not asked for anything in my name. Ask and you will receive, and your joy will be complete.'

Talk in agreement with Jesus about Fred

Yes, just talking to Jesus about Fred is the first step. But talking to Jesus *on your own* is one thing. Talking to Jesus about Fred *in agreement with others* is better yet. If the Bible is right when it says that without faith it is impossible to please God, then it is reasonable to conclude that faith pleases God. But it seems that faith when stated in agreement is especially pleasing.

Four friends brought their paralysed friend to Jesus. The guy might have been squealing and kicking all the way for all I know, except that he was paralysed so he probably only screamed. But in any event, there is nothing to suggest that he had any faith of his own. There were too many people for them to be able to get close to Jesus in the conventional manner. So they climbed up on to the roof, punched a hole and dumped him at Jesus' feet. Jesus looked up and saw four expectant faces peering down at him through the roof: 'When he saw their faith he said to the paralysed man, "Your sins are forgiven."' Faith by proxy. Faith in agreement; a useful precedent.

Actually it's more than a precedent. It's a promise of Jesus: 'Again, I tell you that if two of you on earth agree about anything you ask for, it will be done for you by my Father in heaven.'

The picture of four lads manhandling their friend up a drainpipe and then through a hole in a roof is a wonderful picture of agreed teamwork. There can't have been too much: 'Are you sure this is a good idea? I don't think we should be doing this. Surely if Jesus wanted our friend to walk, he would have given him legs.' Neither do I imagine them fighting between themselves. It would only have taken one to stamp off in a rage and the poor fellow would have been dumped. And I don't see them making contingency plans for what to do if nothing happened. 'Now if Jesus just ignores him, or even if he tries to heal and nothing happens, I'll shout "Fire!" and when everyone runs out, we'll go in and grab him back.' Faith has no back doors. They had no other plan but Jesus' grace.

Dan and Dorothy are Catholics. We have in common an English ancestry, and both Joy and Dorothy are nurses. Dan and I enjoy the TV series *All Creatures Great and Small* and the occasional game of golf.

I had banged this drum about agreed prayer for a while and felt it was high time I practised what I preached. So one evening after James Herriot had done his thing, we suggested that we ought to start meeting regularly to pray for our neighbours. We agreed a time when we could spend half an hour – not a whole evening, just a slot.

We prayed by name for the residents of the four houses adjoining our property and they did likewise. Most people who write about this kind of thing in books tell how they rose at 4.30 in the morning and prayed specifically for five years. Well, we didn't. We met at 7:00 p.m. for twenty minutes and we only kept it up for six weeks! Then it fizzled out, falling victim to some other more pressing matter.

A year later we had occasion to be watching another episode of *All Creatures*. Once again my conscience attacked me. 'We ought to start a Christian group for our neighbours.'

'Your house or ours?' Dan and Dorothy readily agreed.

We settled for their house because it had a better living-room than ours, and invited everyone who lived in their street, twenty-five households. Dan and Dorothy were amazed to find that three of their immediate neighbours were interested. These were people whose names we knew well, though we had never met them. They were all people for whom we had prayed by name on six inconsistent occasions.

Agreed prayer in Jesus' name! Jesus promised, so it can't hurt to try it!

Talk with Jesus about Fred

It is important to talk *with* Jesus about Fred, not merely to talk *to* him. 'With' implies that it is a dialogue, not just a monologue. Perhaps Jesus has something to say to you about Fred. Prayer is not intended to be a one-way street. Sometimes I talk so much in the presence of God that he would need to interrupt me if he wanted to get a word in edgeways.

When young Samuel, a fledgling prophet, first heard the voice of God, he mistook it for that of his boss, Eli. But as years went by he developed the skill of recognising when it was God who was speaking to him.

The prophet Isaiah shared that the secret of his ability to speak God's word to weary people was his time each morning spent listening to God's word. 'The Sovereign Lord has given me an instructed tongue, to know the word that sustains the weary.

He wakens me morning by morning, wakens my ear to listen like one being taught. The Sovereign Lord has opened my ears.' If I could only learn to listen, then perhaps I might glean a word from God to sustain weary old Fred.

Jeremiah railed against his contemporary prophets who spoke without first listening to God. He spoke of a tuning in process, the ability to home in on the voice of God. 'Who has stood in the council of the Lord to perceive and to hear his word, or who has given heed to his word and listened?'

There is a progression – perceive . . . hear . . . give heed . . . listen.

Conduct an experiment. Put the book down and just listen. What can you hear? Try to discern the noises that are audible to you. First you'll *perceive* a sound as you become conscious of it for the first time. It was probably there all the time, but you had blanked it out in your concentration on this fascinating book! Now that you've identified it, you can *hear* it easily. Next, you *give heed* to it, you concentrate on it. Where is it coming from? What is making that sound? Finally you *listen* to it, maybe moving closer so the sound becomes clearer. Is it something you should respond to? – a dripping tap that needs a new washer, a cat scratching on the door wanting to get out, or even an ominous silence that suggests that your child is doing something naughty!

Is it possible that Jesus has something to say to you about your friend? You have been so busy talking to him about Fred that you have blanked out Jesus' voice speaking to you.

There is a strange parable that Jesus told on the subject of prayer. It runs like this: You receive unexpected guests late at night and are embarrassed by an empty refrigerator. So you go to your neighbour's house, bang on the door and ask for the loan of three loaves of bread so you can at least make some sandwiches. The neighbour shouts from within that he is already in bed and that you are disturbing his children's beauty sleep. But you go on banging on the door until eventually he gets up and gives you the bread, not because he's a good neighbour but just to get some peace and quiet.

The moral of the story is to persist in prayer. My problem with the story is that it suggests that God is like a bad neighbour who will only answer prayer if you pester him long enough! But suppose the parable were to be understood the other way round. Suppose you were the one in bed asleep, unwilling to have the needs of your neighbours rock your boat or invade your dreams. And suppose it was God standing at the door knocking and calling out: 'Lend me three loaves of bread for I have this friend (called Fred) and I have no money to set before him but that which is in your bank account, no arms with which to hug him but your arms, no shoulder for him to cry on but your shoulder.' I fear that God is far more ready to answer my prayers than I am to listen to his voice prompting me about my friend's needs.

So we are through with talking about Fred behind his back. He is back in the room now and there are the three of you sitting at your kitchen table. Fred is only aware of you, but you know Jesus is sitting opposite Fred, across the table. And there is a mutual sense of expectancy between you and Jesus, for you have talked together about Fred, and now here he is, sitting at table with you both! It's time to bring Fred into the conversation.

Ask Fred what he wants Jesus to do for him

I am impressed by the way Jesus always met people at their point of need. He didn't say to the blind man: 'What you need is a New International Version of the Bible,' because he knew that he wouldn't be able to read it. He didn't offer a new pair of trainers to the lame man at the pool of Bethesda. He didn't tell the crowds by the lake that they needed the bread of life until he had shared out among them the five loaves and two fish. He met people where they were.

I fear that I tend to ignore my friend's agenda and lay on him my own. I am always trying to get him to attend church or read a good Christian book or become a Christian, when what Fred really wants is someone with whom he can play a round of golf; what he needs is a loan to tide him over to next month; he could really use a hand fixing his lawn mower.

I fear I may have convinced Fred that the only thing Jesus is interested in as far as he is concerned is church, reading stuffy books and having weird religious experiences. Jesus knows nothing about golf, money or lawn mowers, neither is he interested in learning!

So there you are at your kitchen table. Fred says to you, 'You know I am really worried about my lad. He's just not doing as well in school as I know he should be. I think he's mixing with the wrong crowd. And I can't help noticing that he never seems to look me in the eye any more, like he used to.'

You could reply that he needs to repent of his sin and to be converted, and you could give him a tract to read over with his son when he gets home. Or worse, you could tell him how wonderful your teenagers are and how they all attend church and Sunday School every week and never give you any problems.

On the other hand, you could identify with his problem and admit your own worries in that area. And you could add something along these lines: 'You know Fred, I greatly appreciate your friendship and I try to make it a habit to pray for you every day. Sometimes I am not sure what I should be praying about, so would you mind if I prayed for your son?'

I would be very surprised if he told you to mind your own damn business and to keep your religion to yourself! You see, you would have met Fred at his point of need. You would have fed into his mind the thought, the very true thought, that Jesus really cares about his son. His agenda is the same as Jesus' agenda. Religion is not therefore a department of life sealed off from reality, a hobby that some strange people indulge in on Sunday mornings. Jesus cares about parent/teenager relationships, and specifically *Fred's* relationship with *Fred's* son.

And there's another thing. You have been praying for Fred for some time now. You have also been

asking Jesus to speak to you about Fred's needs.
Is this conversation Jesus' answer to your prayer?
Don't imagine that you are the only person who
prays. Most people pray when they get worried, even
those who make no pretence of being a Christian.
I'll lay odds that Fred prays too, as he tosses and
turns at night, unable to sleep through worry about
his son.

Worry is God's knock. He challenges the complacent
who say, 'I'm rich, prosperous and need nothing,'
this way: 'Those I love I rebuke and chasten . . .
Look, it's me. I stand at the door and knock . . .' God
knocks at a man's point of need. A man recognises his
point of need by worry. His response to God's knock
is his response to worry – prayer. 'Be anxious for
nothing, but . . . let your requests be made known
to God.' So if you want to know the point at which
God is seeking access to a man's life, identify what
he is worried about and the chances are that if you
listen carefully, you may discern the sound of God
knocking.

Your promise to pray for Fred's son may well tie
up in Fred's mind with his secret prayer to God in
the night.

Lillian was sitting at home one afternoon when a
knock came at the door. There were two young ladies
she had never met before. 'We're from the church
just up the street,' they explained. 'We're praying for
this neighbourhood, but we want to be specific in our
prayer requests. Is there anything special that you are
wanting God to do for you so we can pray with you
about that?' Lillian was impressed. Strangers who

called at her door usually wanted to sell something, or perhaps were collecting money for some worthy cause or trying to push their brand of religion. But these girls seemed to be interested in what was on her mind. And what impressed her so much was that she did have something on her mind that worried her very much. Her marriage was breaking up. She had been awake much of the previous night worrying about it, and finally, remembering her childhood Sunday School, she had prayed about it. She had woken up that morning with the expectancy that someone would call who might be able to help her. She expected it to be the Jehovah's Witnesses, for they often called. But no. It was two girls asking what she was praying about. God was knocking at Lillian's door through her marriage and through two girls.

Six weeks later, I was talking to one of the local pastors. He told me that he had been alone in his church one afternoon when he heard a knocking sound coming from a side door. He went to investigate and found Lillian standing there. She explained that she had tried several churches, but they were all locked and she had got no response to her knocking. His was the last church she was going to try. So the conclusion to the story is no surprise. Lillian came into the church and Jesus came into her heart. The issue of her marriage is not yet resolved as far as I know, otherwise I could say: 'They all lived happily ever after'. But this is no fairy tale.

So there you sit, you and Fred and Jesus. Fred is

worried about his son and you have promised to pray for him.

Let Fred tell you exactly what he wants Jesus to do for him

Fred may not yet be ready to address his worry directly to Jesus. All Fred has done to this point is to tell you what is worrying him. And anyway, worry is not faith. So take the conversation a step further.

You have asked Fred's permission to let you pray for his son, and he replies: 'I should be most grateful if you would.' Now ask him something like this: 'Fred, tell me specifically what you want Jesus to do about the situation.'

'What do you want Jesus to do for you?' implies that Jesus can do something to help

By asking that question you have made room for the original positive thought to grow. Not only is Jesus interested in Fred's agenda, but he may actually be able to do something about the problem.

'What do you want Jesus to do for you?' directs Fred's attention to Jesus, not to your prayers

If you had asked him: 'Fred, what do you want me to pray about for you?' you would have drawn his attention to you and your praying ability. That's not what you want at all. You want him to look to Jesus for the answer, not to your prayers. I know that may seem like splitting hairs, but there is a vital difference. You want him to talk to Jesus directly, not through you as a go-between. And when the answer comes, you want him to be grateful to Jesus, not to you for your effective praying. And next time he has a need, you want him to go directly to Jesus himself, rather than coming back to you asking that you give Jesus another message from him.

How often do we hear: 'Your prayers have saved the day. But for your praying, I don't like to think what would have happened!' So who is getting the credit, the one who prays or Jesus? Therefore, ask Fred: 'What do you want *Jesus* to do about the situation?'

It may be that Fred will be slow in answering your question. Don't try and put words into his mouth or his answer will be meaningless. However, you can help things along a little. By asking Fred what he wants God to do for him, you have asked him to bare his soul, to make himself vulnerable. I hesitate to be that open. So help him by making yourself vulnerable. Share with him something close to your heart that is on your mind. Tell him about some answer to prayer that you have recently received. Even ask him to pray for something that is troubling you.

The key that once cracked things open with some of our neighbours was my wife's vulnerability. One of our teenagers had been out all night and Joy was terribly worried. I was away speaking somewhere, so

Joy went over to our next-door neighbours who made no pretence of being Christian. Joy burst into tears. 'I need help,' she sobbed. 'Please pray for me.' To her surprise the neighbour did, there and then! Not only that, but she started to open up about her own worries about her child!

It is so important never to give the impression that we Christians have a monopoly on prayer!

'What do you want Jesus to do for you?' is the way Jesus himself drew faith from those he met

Bartimaeus the blind beggar sits on the outskirts of Jericho shouting his head off to catch Jesus' attention. When Jesus at last sends for him, he comes tapping up to Jesus with his white cane, 'gravel blind' written all over his face. But Jesus still asks the question: 'What do you want me to do for you?' The problem was as obvious as the nose on his face, and to cap it all Jesus was God and knew everything anyway. So why did he ask? Answer: because he wanted to hear the man's reply. Why should you ask Fred what he wants? Because Jesus wants to hear his reply. Bartimaeus responded: 'Lord, I want to see!' Jesus heard what he said and took it as an expression of faith. 'Receive your sight! Your faith has made you well.' There is no mention of faith. Jesus didn't ask on this occasion: 'Do you believe I can give you sight?' He just recognised the man's statement of want as a statement of faith.

So how will Fred respond to your question? His reply will be an embryonic statement of faith, and embryos have a habit of growing. It is unlikely that Fred will say: 'I want my son to suddenly become an A student, to become a glowing Christian who will dedicate his life to the alleviation of world poverty.' Embryos aren't that big! More likely he will say something like: 'I would just like to be able to talk to him, like I used to.'

The size of a man's 'want' indicates the size of his embryonic faith.

A street worker in Vancouver told me of an interesting incident which illustrates my point. He met a middle-aged, down-at-heel gentleman in the red-light district of town. He was obviously crippled and walked with difficulty with the aid of a cane. The worker took him to McDonald's and bought him a meal. At some point in the meal my friend offered to pray for the man, an offer readily accepted. When asked, 'What do you want God to do for you?' the man had no reply. 'Well, would you like God to help you find a place to live?' prompted my friend.

'Yes, I would like that.'

'And would you like him to help you get work?'

'Yes, I really do want a job.'

'Would you like him to heal your leg?'

'No,' said the man sadly. 'I don't think even God could do that for me.'

So how big was the embryo? What could my friend pray for in a kind of 'be it to you according to your faith' manner? The answer is clear. The embryonic faith of this man stretched to a wish that God would find him a home and a job, but did not extend to healing for his leg.

It's Fred's faith that we are seeking to work with.

So we take such faith as he can express and help it to grow. We don't trouble our heads about what he does not yet believe. Patience!

'What do you want Jesus to do for you?' calls for a response from the will, not the intellect

What a person wants and what a person believes are closely allied, as I have already said. Arguments tend to centre on what people do not want, and therefore have very little to do with faith. Yet how often do we try to help people to faith by starting an argument! I have spent hours in debate with atheists and agnostics, and most of that time was fruitless. Arguments create more heat than light and all they do is dig the trenches deeper and confirm each side in the opinions they held before the argument started. But now there is an element more powerful than logic which confirms each in his opinion – pride. It is a matter of honour, not right and wrong. As far as I can see from Scripture, Paul's debate on Mars Hill in Athens resulted in less than revival. Some mocked, others procrastinated, though there was a little fruit.

I met a man recently while door-knocking, cold turkey. 'Good morning, I'm representing the church up the road,' I greeted the elderly man when eventually he responded to my knocking. A pause while we exchanged small talk. At least he didn't close the door on me. 'As a church we are praying for the community and we are trying to find out what the real needs of this town are. So could I ask you two questions?' He agreed, so I continued: 'What do you want God to do for this town?'

'Well . . .' he said expansively. 'Actually I'm an atheist, so I don't quite know how to answer your question. What makes you think your religion is the right one, anyway?'

That could have triggered an argument, but I avoided the pitfall. 'I'm not here to debate religion. Everyone is entitled to their own opinion. But what I want to know is what help you think our town needs from God.'

'That's what I mean. What gives you the right to come knocking on my door, forcing your religion down my throat?'

I assured him again that forcing religion down anybody's throat was certainly not on my agenda. Eventually he declined to answer the question but, 'You said there was a second question. Why don't you try that one?'

'Well, the other question is very like the first one and I don't think you'd like it any better.'

'Try me!'

'What do you want God to do for you personally? But you're an atheist so I'll write down "Nothing", shall I?'

'Well, wait a minute! I wouldn't say that.'

'If you don't believe in God's existence, how could you have a request for him?'

'I suppose I could ask him for ten more years of health and strength.'

I am not suggesting that the man was instantly converted, or that his request was a great statement of faith. But I am saying that in drawing that longing

out of him and by laying it alongside the possibility
that God just might exist, I did more to foster faith
in him than engaging in an argument or debate. His
will was a bridge for faith, while an argument would
certainly have acted as a ditch.

'Faith is the assurance of things hoped for . . .'
Note the 'hoped for'. If you invite someone to
trust God for something they don't want anyway,
where is the motivation to believe? 'Trust in God
so you can become a Christian!' but if the person
views Christianity as hypocritical nonsense, where
is the incentive for faith? Faith is certainly not 'the
assurance of things you despise'! Faith assures a
person's hopes and works alongside his will.

There are, however, some people who really do
want the right things, who are hungry to know God.
The things they 'hope for' are very positive and
godly. The embryo of their faith is well developed.
One such was a young lady I met on that same
visitation programme. She was in her mid-twenties.
I don't recall how she answered the first question, but
when I asked her what she wanted God to do for her
personally, her eyes filled with tears. 'My husband
is a Christian and I am not. So what I would like God
to do for me is to give me faith, so I can believe in
him. Then my husband and I could be in agreement
again.' She wanted the assurance of that for which
she only dared hope. She asked for faith.

'What do you want Jesus to do for you?' tells you what you should be praying about

If you don't ask the question, how else will you

know what to pray for? Some people pray based on a word of knowledge, yet Jesus, who is omniscient, rarely operated that way. He asked the question and listened carefully to the reply.

I remember one person telling me about a sick grandmother, who was ninety-six years old. What should I pray, I wondered: 'O God, raise her up from the bed of sickness and give her another fifty years of health and strength!'?

So I probed: 'What do you want God to do for her?'

'I just want her to die peacefully, without suffering.' There was the substance for my prayer, in tune with the person's will, and clearly the right thing to ask.

And Fred has given you the dimensions of his embryonic faith which you can use as the substance for your prayer. 'I would just like to be able to talk to him, like I used to.'

Now it's time to bring Jesus into the conversation.

Talk to Jesus with Fred about Fred's agenda

'Fred, I can understand how worried you must be about your son. I will pray for him, and specifically that you will be able to talk to him openly, man to man.'

'That is kind of you. It helps just to know you care.'

'Why don't we pray together about the situation, right now?'

'I'm not much of a praying man, myself.'

'Well, fine. I'm not much good at praying either. But I reckon God is good at listening. I'll pray first and then you can pray, if you want to.'

Without giving Fred time to become embarrassed you dive right into a simple prayer: 'Father, you understand how worried Fred is about his son. We pray that you will protect him and give Fred an opportunity for a good heart-to-heart talk with him in the near future. We ask this in the name of the Lord Jesus Christ.'

In praying like this you will have helped Fred in a number of ways.

Praying out loud makes Jesus real

For starters you will have given him the most vivid illustration that Jesus really is present. You see, you can theorise about a situation; you can talk about a person until the cows come home. But a one-minute conversation with that person turns the whole thing from theory to reality. By talking to Jesus directly in Fred's company you will accomplish more than talking all day to Fred about Jesus.

Praying out loud breaks the sound barrier

Fred may never have heard anyone pray like that before. Any prayers he may have heard were probably vague, unrelated and in old-fashioned English. To hear someone he knows speaking in plain language about things that are on his mind and using his name personally is likely to make a real impression.

Don't misunderstand me. I am not suggesting that you can manipulate Fred by putting on a performance. What I am saying is that for Fred to overhear a genuine prayer on his behalf may be a very moving experience for him, one that is likely to foster faith in him.

Praying out loud is what Jesus himself did to help those who listened in

Jesus set the precedent for this kind of thing. A friend of his, by the name of Lazarus, took sick and died. Had Jesus been quicker off the mark he might have arrived at his bedside in time to heal him, but it seems Jesus deliberately dragged his feet. Doubtless Jesus could also save us from a lot of grief by intervening in our affairs before anything nasty should shatter our peace. But in the case of Lazarus there was something more important for the rest of the family to learn, something that Jesus considered worth the price of four days of mourning. They needed to learn faith. Faith is what we are seeking to foster in Fred.

When Jesus first arrived at the front door of the bereaved household, Martha tore strips off him for being late for the funeral, let alone the sickbed. Jesus responded with this: 'I am the resurrection and the life; he who believes in me, though he die yet shall he live, and whoever lives and believes in me shall never die. Do you believe this?'

'Yes, Lord,' replied Martha. 'I believe that you are the Christ, the Son of God.' Note that she believed *who* Jesus was rather than *how* he was going to solve the problem.

Later on, at the graveside, Jesus asked that the grave be opened. Martha objected on the practical grounds that her brother had been dead for four days and by now would stink of decay.

'Did I not tell you that if you would believe you would see the glory of God?'

So Jesus did something that was deliberately designed to help Martha and others to have faith. Standing in front of the open grave, which clearly was the felt point of need for all present, Jesus prayed out loud. His prayer was not designed to manipulate the family and their fellow mourners, but it was a genuine prayer spoken out loud, more for the benefit of the human audience than for the ears of God the Father. Here's what he said: 'Father, I thank you that you have heard me. Actually I know that you always hear me, but I have said this (out loud) on account of the people standing by, that they may believe that you sent me.'

Next moment Lazarus is restored alive to his family.

So if Jesus prayed aloud, deliberately so that he would be overheard by those around him for the specific purpose of fostering faith in them, then that is a good enough precedent for us to do the same!

The sky was black and the rain was just about to deluge on to the highway when I spotted an eager hitch-hiker with his pack at his feet and his thumb extended towards Vancouver, where I was headed. I pulled over, muttering a quick prayer for him. He threw his pack into the back seat and climbed in gratefully just as the first large drops hit.

'Hell,' he said. 'I prayed to God it wouldn't rain!'

That was too good an opening to miss. 'Do you do that often?' I enquired.

'Do what?'

'Pray to God?'

'Not often, but I do from time to time.'

We discussed the weather for a while, then we returned to the subject of his spasmodic praying. 'What sort of things do you pray about?' I asked.

'The last time I can remember praying was last night. I have just been out hiking in the mountains. I was way up above the snow line all alone when I came across some fresh bear tracks. I prayed then!'

'And what sort of thing is on your mind at the moment, that you want God to do for you?'

'Well, I'm not sure.'

'Suppose you were sitting in this car next to God and he said to you: "Steve, what do you want me to do for you?" What would you ask?'

He thought for a long moment, just as anyone might give careful thought if their fairy godmother offered three wishes. It would be a crime to blow the opportunity! Then he said: 'Well, to tell you the truth, I am really bothered about young people, about my age, who are on the streets with no place to call home. I would like to be able to do something to help them. Maybe I could become a famous rock star so I could make a lot of money and then be able to offer them something really good.'

So what should I make of that as a prayer request?

I picked out what I could. 'Steve, I think it is wonderful that you are concerned for homeless young people. I am sure God shares your concern. Why don't we ask him together to use you in some way?'

'What, now? Here?'

'Yes! I'll pray and you can too, if you want to. I promise not to close my eyes!'

I started right in: 'Dear Father, Steve is concerned about all the young people who are homeless in this city. Please would you give Steve such a wonderful experience of yourself that he will have something really good to offer to kids in need. In the name of the Lord Jesus Christ.' Well, it wasn't exactly what he had asked for, but it was close enough!

Steve didn't pray. He just gaped at me. Eventually he said: 'I can't believe you did that!'

'Did what?' I countered innocently.

'Well, preached, or whatever you did.'

'I didn't preach. I merely prayed, and anyone can do that.'

'I just never heard anything like that in my entire life. Thank you. It was wonderful.'

I set him down by McDonald's and watched him walking away across the car park, shaking his head and muttering: 'I don't believe he did that . . .'

Praying out loud models how to pray

Remember my difficulty in addressing Lady Salisbury? Jesus taught his disciples more about prayer by actually praying a model prayer than by any other method. 'When you pray, say . . .' Then followed a prayer out loud, dubbed 'The Lord's Prayer'.

What could Steve have learned about prayer from my prayer for him?

How do you address God? – *Father*
What kind of thing can you pray about? – *Whatever is on your mind*
Do you have to use Latin or old English? – *No. Plain speech is fine*
How should you sign off or say goodbye at the end of the conversation? – *In Jesus' name*

Now that is not an exhaustive lesson on prayer but it is enough to get someone started.

Praying out loud is an expression of contagious faith

Faith is more often caught than taught. There is something about seeing a friend praying to God in simple confidence that is catching. Worry is contagious, but faith is more so.

The very first student mission I undertook was in Goldsmith's College in south-east London. I approached the week with fear and trepidation. I didn't do too well in school so I assumed that any one of the students I encountered would be far more intelligent than I am.

On the Monday morning, the first morning of the mission, I took time to sit around the foyer of the

college. There I could watch the students coming
and going. I wanted to catch something of the
atmosphere of the place, and perhaps absorb some
of the intellectual aura!

Sitting on a bench was a young lady with huge
round pink-tinged spectacles. She was reading a very
clever-looking book, the title of which I couldn't
even understand, let alone the contents. But I had
to start somewhere, so I moved over and sat next to
her.

'Good morning,' I started. 'Have you heard about
"New Life"?'

'"New Life"?' she repeated. 'What's that?'

'The Christian Union are putting on a week of
special lectures.'

'What's it all about?'

'It's all about God.'

'Oh well, I'm an agnostic, you see. I wouldn't be
interested.'

Now I don't know any Greek, but I have heard
lots of sermons from learned people who do. So I
pulled some out in the hope that Greek wasn't her
second subject.

'I'm sorry to hear you are an agnostic.'

'Why is that?'

'Because the word "agnostic" is derived from
the Greek word which means "ignorance". And
if I were you I wouldn't want to sit in the foyer
of this august institution and admit that I was an
ignoramus.'

She didn't appreciate that, I could tell, for her
face flushed as pink as her glasses. Coolly she
retorted: 'I merely meant to say that I don't believe

in God, and therefore I will not be interested in your lectures.'

'Oh, you don't believe in God. So you are an atheist. You are convinced there is no God.'

'I didn't go so far as to say that. I just don't think God exists.'

'So it is just possible that God does exist?'

'Yes, I suppose so.'

'Have you ever asked him?'

'Have I ever asked who what?'

'God, if he exists. After all, the God who may or may not exist promises to answer prayer. Simple logic would suggest that the best way to find out is to ask him if he's real.'

'Maybe you're right. Perhaps I'll do that sometime.'

'No!' I blundered on. 'Let's do it right now. I do believe in God, so I'll talk first, then you can say what you want to.'

I discovered her name was Anne and then pitched straight in: 'Father, I do believe in you and am convinced that you hear me now. Anne doesn't believe. I pray that you will show her not only that you are real, but also just how much you love her. In the name of the Lord Jesus Christ . . .' And turning to Anne, 'Now it's your turn.'

There was a long pause. Anne glanced around to make sure no one was within earshot. Her face was now very white! Only the glasses retained any colour. 'O God, I don't think you are real . . . But if you are there, I would like to know about it. Amen.'

There was no echoey voice, no bolt of lightning, so we parted company.

About five o'clock that afternoon I chanced to bump into her in another part of the college. 'Hey, you're the guy I was talking to this morning, about God. Well, you won't believe this. I've just phoned my parents in Manchester and told them that I am thinking about becoming religious. Where are the lectures you were talking about?'

I told her and she came, and before she went to bed that night she too believed.

Yes, God had answered her prayer. And something else. She had caught my faith. Prayer expressed out loud as an expression of faith is highly contagious.

Praying out loud you proclaim Jesus' name

When the name of God is proclaimed, he is there even though you cannot see him. The evidence of your ears is more convincing than that of the eyes when it comes to fostering faith. 'Faith comes by hearing . . .'

Of course, God who is omnipresent is there all the time, yet in the examples I gave in the last chapter it seems that when the name of God was proclaimed those within earshot became particularly conscious of the presence of God, so much so that they fell down in worship or jumped up, healed.

On my way to speak at a camp on one of the many islands off the west coast of British Columbia, I fell into conversation with a worried-looking man in his twenties. We were both leaning over the rail of the little car ferry taking us on the twenty-minute crossing. The sun was setting behind us and the wind was catching the spray and whipping it off the white caps. I told him I was on my way to Pioneer Pacific, a Christian youth camp. He brightened. 'Oh, really? I'm going to a Christian camp too, Camp Columbia. It's a camp for Anglican lay youth workers. I really don't know how I got into this.'

I asked him to elaborate on his misgivings. 'I like young people and I want to help them, but I'm not sure what I have to offer them,' he told me.

'But you have Jesus.'

'I suppose so. I have attended church all my life. But it all seems so irrelevant, so removed from where the kids are at.'

I suggested we should pray for each other. 'Would you pray that I will know exactly what I should say to the youngsters at Pioneer Pacific? And what do you want God to do for you?'

'I think I would like him to show me something that I can offer to lonely, lost young people.'

He prayed silently for a few moments, then I pitched in. 'Dear Father, I ask you this weekend to so take hold of John that he may be assured of your presence. Please become so real to him that as he speaks to lonely youngsters it may be as though he held them in one hand and you in the other. So may he put their hand into yours. In the name of the Lord Jesus Christ.'

Suddenly that little ferry boat seemed to be sailing right past the gates of heaven. The presence of God was there. John was quite overcome.

Who has seen the wind?
Neither you nor I.
But when the trees bow down their heads
the wind is passing by.

Who has seen God? Neither you nor I. But when the name of Jesus is proclaimed, you know he's passing by. 'The wind blows wherever it pleases. You hear its sound, but you cannot tell where it comes from or where it is going. So it is with everyone born of the Spirit.'

But some may ask: 'What happens if you pray for someone and nothing happens?' I think if Peter and John had asked themselves that question on their way into the Temple when faced with the cripple, the Church would never have got off the ground. Doubtless they would have contented themselves with a tract and an invitation to church next weekend!

Martin Luther described faith as 'a reckless, daring confidence in God'. That kind of faith is worth catching. The stay-at-home kind of faith, which never takes any risks, cuts no ice and isn't worth catching anyway.

What happens if Jesus doesn't show in answer to your prayer? That's his problem. Your job is not to defend his reputation or to play it so safe that if he never showed, no one would notice! Your job is to be faithful, and 'faithful' means 'full of faith' worth catching. Fred needs to catch faith.

Back to the thought of Fred, still sitting in your

kitchen. You have talked to Jesus about Fred. You have talked to Fred about Jesus, specifically about Jesus' interest in Fred's needs. You have asked Fred what he wants Jesus to do for him. He has told you he would like Jesus to enable him to have a good talk with his son, and you have passed on the request to Jesus, with Fred listening in. All that remains is for Fred to get into conversation with Jesus direct, and you have achieved your initial objective. You will have got them talking to each other.

Let Fred talk to Jesus

I have prayed aloud with many uncertain people. Lots of them have then added their own faltering prayer, directed straight to Jesus. Others have remained silent. Yet the importance of offering the opportunity cannot be overstressed. 'Fred, let's pray now together for your son. I'll pray first, then you pray if you want to.'

I was driving out of the city of Victoria, on the west coast of Canada, on my way to a Bible school, where I was due to be teaching for the week. Just beyond the last traffic lights, before the freedom of the open road, there stood a hitch-hiker. So I pulled over. Rob was from Montreal, Quebec, and very far from home. He had just been to visit his brother for the first time in a number of years, and the reunion had not been a happy one. His family was scattered all over the country; his father was dead and he missed his mother. All this I learned as we reached the start of the scenic Malahat Drive. He had had a beer or two which had served to loosen his tongue.

'Do you ever pray?' I dropped in out of the blue.

It didn't throw him. 'Yes, as a matter of fact I do. My mother gave me a book of prayers and I sometimes read them.'

Now books of prayers can be very helpful, but I wanted to lead him on. 'When you talk to your mother, presumably you use a book of sayings?'

'A book of sayings!' he repeated. 'Why would I need a book of sayings when I talk to my mother?' I could see out of the corner of my eye that he was looking at me as if I was an alien. 'No, of course I don't!'

'Then how do you know what to talk about?'

'That's easy. I just tell her whatever is on my mind.'

'Then why is it that when you talk to your heavenly Father you need a book of prayers to tell you what to say?'

'I never really thought about it.'

'No one ever told you that you could talk to God about anything that is on your heart?'

'No, they didn't.'

'Well, you can.'

There was a long pause while I let that sink in. The road was reaching the top of a long climb, and the land fell away steeply to the right of the road down into the blue of the ocean far below.

'Rob, if God had picked you up and he was sitting here in the car next to you and he turned to you and said: "Rob, what do you want me to do for you?", what would you ask for?'

He thought very carefully before answering my question, probably jumping through the old fairy godmother hoop like the last hitch-hiker! But when he spoke it was slow and deliberate: 'I would ask him for a family, a close family that stayed together and loved each other. That is what I would ask God to do for me.'

So far it was still in the abstract world of 'what I *would* ask God for'. I wanted to know if he *was* asking God for that.

'Well, Rob, do you want God to do that for you? God loves families and that is just the kind of request that I feel sure he is in the business of granting.'

'Yes. That is exactly what I do want God to do for me.'

'Then let's ask him to do that right now. I'll pray first, then if you want to pray too just go ahead.' He nodded.

'Dear Father, in you all families in heaven and on earth are blessed. I ask you to give Rob a close happy family. I pray that you will give him a lovely girl who will become his wife and will be faithful to him all their lives. Please give them lots of children who will love their mother and father. Please would you become the centre of this family so that your love will hold them all together. In the name of the Lord Jesus Christ.'

I didn't say any more, for I felt a tremendous sense of the presence of God with us in the car. After perhaps a minute, Rob started to pray.

'God, please give me a family just like that. And I do want you to be part of our family, so

I suppose I ought to ask you to come into my life . . .'

I don't know where he got that part about asking God into his life; maybe from another conversation somewhere, or maybe the Holy Spirit prompted him to 'pray as he ought'. But there were tears on his cheeks when he finished, and on mine.

The Malahat slipped away behind us and I put him down in the next town. He hadn't prayed the sinner's prayer or responded to an altar call or completed a decision card, but I left him with the calm assurance that he was on good speaking terms with Jesus.

Once or twice, as I recounted that story, people would ask me about follow-up. 'Surely you linked him up with local Christians?' they would ask askance. I never quite knew what to say. That is, I didn't know until four summers later.

I was teaching in Victoria, at a seminar on personal evangelism. Leighton Ford, the well-known evangelist, was there too, taking half the allotted time. Consequently I was nervous, for he knows more about evangelism than I ever will. As part of my presentation I used this story about Rob. Blow me down if someone didn't come up with the question about follow-up. What would Dr Ford think of one so disorganised? I confessed my weakness and shortcoming to the assembled throng. A lady got to her feet.

'I met Rob, just last week. I asked him how he had become a Christian and he told me some guy with an English accent had given him a ride over the Malahat Drive. He had prayed with him for a family and he had asked Jesus into his life!'

'How's he getting on?' I enquired. 'It's four years since I saw him.'

'Just fine,' the lady assured me. 'He's walking with Jesus.'

5

Body Language

It's better to get the church into the neighbourhood than to get a neighbour to church

I used to host a regular weekly TV chat show. I suppose that made me a televangelist! I did it on behalf of the association of churches in our town of White Rock, British Columbia. Of course, it was hardly nationwide coverage, being just a local cable network which reached fewer than fifty thousand people, assuming the entire population tuned in to watch, a fact which I very much doubt. It was a phone-in format in which I would start by interviewing interesting people from the community and would then open the phone lines for questions and comments. You might imagine, therefore, that with a potential audience of fifty thousand the lines would be jammed, but in fact we received very few calls. My wife Joy was a regular caller, but eventually people grew suspicious of the mystery lady with the English accent who called in every week, pretending not to know me.

Immediately following my show was a psychic phone-in chat show. Pat was the host, and her guests ranged from witches to metaphysicians who would dole out advice to callers based on wisdom from the stars. It galled me to see that the phone lines were always jammed for her hour, but not for mine.

So I asked her one day: 'Pat, it seems grossly unfair that I, who consult Almighty God for wisdom, am virtually ignored by the community, while you are swamped by calls for advice that is derived from rocks and crystals and the movement of the heavenly bodies. Why is that?'

'It's quite simple,' she responded. 'People perceive you and the Church in general to be irrelevant. Canadians are just not interested in religion, church services, hymn-singing or even going to heaven when they die. To them, all the grand churches scattered around our community are so much wasted space.'

'Come off it, Pat. The Church is involved in lots of wonderful community programmes. It isn't all bad.'

'No. You're missing my point. I'm not saying that the Church is irrelevant, just that people perceive it as such. They have no wish to become involved in activities or a lifestyle that seems to be out of touch with the real world. I fear that until you Christians learn to be good neighbours by getting out of your beautiful churches and into the neighbourhood, you will continue to be perceived as irrelevant.'

I wouldn't have minded her saying all that, except that she was so right!

Too busy in church to love our neighbour

Cam was a Methodist pastor, struggling to establish a new congregation in Abbotsford, near Vancouver. On Sunday mornings he rented the building of a Seventh Day Adventist church who had little use for their facilities on the first day of the week.

'I just can't get sufficient numbers together for people to feel that we are rolling. What can we do?' he asked me.

'Perhaps the people around here are not interested in religion and see you as irrelevant. Until you get out of your church building and become good neighbours to the people of this neighbourhood, they will continue to ignore you.' I was still smarting from Pat's advice!

I agreed to meet Cam every Wednesday afternoon to visit the homes which surrounded the church. Our objective was to find people who would be interested in being part of a neighbourhood group. We would identify ourselves to the people we visited as representing the church up the road. 'We are trying to establish groups of neighbours who might be interested in getting together to pray for the needs of this neighbourhood and to take action to make it an even better place to live.' Pat would have been proud of me!

Abbotsford is in the Bible belt; in fact it is described as the buckle of the belt. It has a much higher concentration of Christians than in most Canadian cities. In one cul-de-sac containing twenty-five homes we encountered eight Christian families. 'Well, thank you for the invitation, but we are already members of our church and are involved in the choir and a fellowship group. As much as we would like to join a neighbourhood prayer group, we just don't feel we could take anything more on.' Everyone declined.

The only people who showed any interest were non-churchgoers. In fact, in that same cul-de-sac we encountered several people who warmed to the idea of a neighbourhood support group. There was a single mother struggling to instil positive values in her children. There was a benefit claimant who was floundering on the bread line. There was a young lady three weeks off getting married. Her parents were divorced and she was making all the preparations alone. A middle-aged man was struggling with business difficulties, exacerbated no doubt by alcohol, the evidence for which was on his breath.

The last home we visited was perhaps the least friendly. 'Neighbourhood prayer group? You must be kidding! This street is crawling with church-goers, all so busy going to church that they have no time left for being good neighbours.' Pat was right.

So struck was I by that response that I returned to the home of one of the Christians we had encountered and told the lady what had been said. 'And did you know that the lady opposite is a single mother and longs for some help in teaching her children good values? In that home over there, the man is really struggling to make ends meet financially. And the girl next door is getting married in three weeks' time and has no help from her parents or anyone else. Won't you reconsider the idea of some kind of neighbourhood support/prayer group?'

Would you believe it, she still declined. She was

just so busy with her church programme that she had no time left for loving her neighbours.

'Love your neighbour' is what the Bible teaches, but we have sacrificed it in favour of 'Go to church'.

So how do we get the Church back into the neighbourhood?

Get the Church into the neighbourhood, but not in my back yard!

Opposite where I used to live was a vacant five-acre plot. A little truck arrived one day and out jumped a man in a hard hat who proceeded to erect a sign. When he had driven off, I sauntered over to have a look. 'Future site for St Joseph's Church' it read, and showed an artist's impression of a 300-seat sanctuary with Sunday School rooms and a car park which would cover the remainder of the five acres. I suppose you could argue that the church was at last getting into the neighbourhood – my neighbourhood, to be precise.

A week later a worried neighbour rang my bell. 'Have you heard what's planned for over the road? It will ruin our quiet neighbourhood! Something has got to be done to stop it. We are holding an emergency neighbourhood meeting and Judy Higginbottom [our local member of parliament] has agreed to come to help us.'

Now I was in a dilemma, for I knew the pastor who was seeking to plant the church in my neighbourhood. But I couldn't help agreeing that such an imposition would destroy the rural tranquillity of our surroundings. Get the Church into the neighbourhood, but not in my back yard, thank you very much.

The neighbours met and declared war. The church prickled at the thought that they were suffering persecution. The pastor was wise enough to find an alternative site and to my great relief the neighbourhood was preserved.

A neighbourhood church formed from neighbours is one thing. Three hundred people invading someone else's neighbourhood is quite another.

Small fellowship groups work better. Or do they?

A keyhole view of Christians in the neighbourhood

Bill and Lynn phoned me one day. We had never met, but they had heard me preach the previous Sunday and had liked what they heard. 'We need to talk.'

I arrived on Friday evening to find them eating Kentucky Fried Chicken out of a box by the fire. They told me that their daughter had been to a Christian camp in the summer and had been deeply affected, but that a week or so ago she had been involved in a serious motor accident. They had nearly lost her. Bill and Lynn were not religious people, but the whole experience had caused them to attend church last Sunday. 'Tell us, what is all this God stuff about?'

'Do you often attend church?'

'Hardly ever. It all seems so unnecessary.'

'So what do you know about Christianity?'

'We do have some Christians living just over the street. They are nice people, but not terribly friendly. They always seem so busy.'

Bill described what he had observed of 'the Christians' as he dubbed them. 'Every Wednesday evening, about 7.30, a number of cars arrive. The first few are OK, as they fit into the driveway, but the late arrivals have to park out in the street and they mess up the grass verges. And anyway, the kids like to play street hockey and all those cars get in the way. The people all look very serious and hurry into the house with big books under their arms. We often wonder what they do over there. Sometimes we hear some kind of music or singing, but mostly they keep pretty quiet. At 9.45 they all leave. That happens every week. Occasionally they alter the pattern. In September they met once on a Friday night instead, apparently for a barbecue, and we thought we were in for a loud party half the night. But no! They were long gone by 10.00. Can't have had much of a good time to have packed up so early.'

'Are you ever invited to come?' I interjected.

'Once. It was a usual Wednesday evening, but to our surprise we saw all the members coming out on to the street after only half an hour. We watched through the net curtains. They went up and down the street pushing papers into all the letter-boxes. Then they went back inside and finished their gathering at the usual time.'

'So what were the papers about?'

'Oh, just an invitation to attend a "Bible Study".'

And it did assure us that there would be free coffee.'

'Did many of the neighbours attend?'

'Well, we certainly didn't. But we kept an eye out to see who else did go. The usual people arrived from out of the neighbourhood and went inside looking rather nervous. But we didn't see anyone else going, though we did notice a few curtains twitching up and down the street.'

The story does have a happy ending, but I will keep it for later. For now let it suffice to say that somewhere close to the last piece of Kentucky Fried Chicken, Bill and Lynn both received Jesus into their hearts.

Body language requires a body

Fred is my neighbour. To him all this God stuff is totally irrelevant. He doesn't want to put on his best clothes on a Sunday morning and join the religious set singing music that is foreign to him and listening to boring monologues from the pulpit. He doesn't need reminding that he is a sinner. He is already painfully aware of his shortcomings. But the prospect of an hour of being threatened with hell by people no better than himself is one that lacks the necessary motivation to get him out of bed. And anyway, he's not terminally ill, so the assurance of heaven when he dies is as irrelevant to his current thinking as the identity of the winner of the table tennis championship in Beijing!

If I want Fred to get to know Jesus, then Jesus

must present himself to Fred in a manner which is unmistakably relevant. They say that actions speak louder than words. If that is so, then body language is more eloquent than talk.

Body language. Does Jesus have body language? To do so he would need a body.

What a buzz, being one of the original disciples of Jesus. Imagine walking into your home town. 'Jesus, let me introduce you to my friend. He's a leper,' and Jesus would reach out to touch him. 'Here is a blind man, Jesus,' and he would rub mud into his eyes. 'This is my neighbour's daughter, Littleone. She's just died!' Jesus would take her by the hand and raise her. He had hands and arms because he had a body. His body language was eloquent and what it said was deeply relevant to the needs of everyone. Religious people didn't like him much, but they weren't too interested in loving their neighbours.

When Jesus ascended back to heaven, the disciples were lost. There was just them – heads full of memories and a set of revolutionary teachings, but they were alone. Jesus no longer had a body on earth with arms to hug, hands to touch, shoulders to be cried on, knees for kids to sit on, eyes to weep at funerals, feet to go and visit people.

But it quickly became apparent to the disciples that Jesus did still have a body. Them!

Me, you and all of us

And still he has a body today. You. Are those not Jesus' hands that are clutching this book and eagerly

turning the pages? And how about the eyes that are
reading, the ears that are listening, the mind that is
thinking, the wallet that was depleted by the purchase
– to whom do they all belong? 'Do you not know that
your bodies are members of Christ himself?'

So if your body is now the physical, mental and
emotional presence of Jesus, what would happen if
you were to bump into another Christian and there
were two or even three of you? Wouldn't that be
confusing, as though Jesus had a split personality?
Not at all! For the same Jesus lives in other Christians
and 'where two or three come together in my name,
there am I with them,' promised Jesus. The physical,
mental and emotional presence of Jesus becomes
even more tangible, visible and audible.

And what happens when you and your two friends
find yourselves part of a whole congregation, in a
worship service for example? 'The church is his
body, the fullness of him who fills everything in
every way.'

All over the world there are people gathering in
the name of Jesus, millions of us, speaking hundreds
of languages and reflecting multiple cultures. But
we are all together and individually representing the
physical, mental and emotional presence of Jesus.
'You are the body of Christ, and each one of you is
a part of it.'

So what happens when this body of Jesus starts to
act in the name of Jesus, when it meets in his name,
welcomes others in his name, prays in his name,
worships his name, proclaims his name, baptises
in his name? When the name above every name is
proclaimed, the name of Jesus, then God himself is

present and bystanders fall down in worship or jump up, healed.

Oh that this might happen in my neighbourhood, for Fred is my neighbour and Jesus told me to love Fred.

Just imagine ...

The house opposite is empty, until one day a hired van arrives and the new neighbour is moving in. He doesn't have much stuff, so it doesn't take long. No one takes much notice, though there are curtains twitching up and down the street as neighbours take a furtive peep at the latest stranger who dares invade their space. It's just a single guy, no evidence of a family. Probably divorced and running away from his responsibilities. Won't see much of him.

But that's not quite right. Turns out that he is quite the sociable type. First thing he does is to introduce himself. 'Hi. I'm new around here. Good to meet you. Have you lived here long? Nice neighbourhood.' Friendly fellow with a winning smile.

Is that a hockey net in his garage? Perhaps he does have kids, after all, otherwise what would an adult want with a hockey net? But after school he hauls it out into his driveway and appears with his roller blades, a set of pads and a stick. Two or three of the neighbourhood kids join him. How does he know them? That's the Wallace twins, isn't it? He's asking for trouble! Must be the kind who mixes with the wrong people. Where did he get those cakes that the kids are devouring on the front lawn? Must have a wife hidden away some-where!

There it is. The inevitable hot rod! Must be a single guy after all to be able to afford that. He'll spend all his time in his garage and before we know it there will be half a dozen cars in the driveway, all up on blocks with no wheels. Look! He has already got a mate over there, tattoos, can of beer, leaning over the engine, grease up to the armpits. Isn't that Jim Wallace from up the road? Well, that confirms it. This new neighbour is trouble. There will be motorcycle gangs next.

So what's the old lady doing in his car? Must be his mother. No, wait. That's Myrtle Crowther from the tip on the corner. Must be the oldest inhabitant, for she was here long before any of the other houses were even built. Keeps herself to herself and hardly ever comes out. Her house is a disgrace! She hasn't touched her garden in years! It's just a tangle of brambles. And the house! What a ruin! Glass cracked and some windows boarded up altogether; paint peeling from the sills; moss all over the roof. It needs a bulldozer to clear it. Frankly, Myrtle's house lowers the tone of the neighbourhood and certainly must affect property values. It shouldn't be allowed. So what is What's-his-name doing with her in his car?

Oh, so there is a family after all! Look at the three little children peeping out of the living-room window. And here comes the wife, in that rusty old Ford. Listen to that exhaust! Hey, that car is familiar. It belongs to Marg, the single mum three doors down. Those three kids are not her brats, by any chance? Don't tell me he is baby-sitting! Yes, baby-sitting and fixing her exhaust, by the looks of it. What next?

So how come the neighbourhood seems so much more alive recently? Must be ever since What's-his-name moved in over the road. Everyone seems to know each other now. No more driving in and out with scarcely a nod. Must be something to do with that joint garage sale we held. That was a great opportunity to get rid of all our junk. Everyone put all their stuff in their driveway and the big ads that we placed in the local paper brought hundreds of eager buyers. Wasn't that his idea? Must have been, for he was the one who collected the money to help clean up Myrtle's place. And that wasn't so bad, either. Half the neighbourhood got together one Saturday morning for a work party. Oh, what a huge fire! Thought the whole house was going to go up. But by the end of the weekend the garden was cleared and the first coat of paint was on the house, the windows were fixed and the inside was spring-cleaned. Even Myrtle looked scrubbed and smiling. What's-his-name was everywhere.

And then there was the barbecue that we held in the cul-de-sac at the end. I don't know where all the flags came from, but we carted down our own barbecues and took our own lawn chairs. Quite a party!

We have our own street hockey team now, you know – the pride of the neighbourhood! The kids are all keen and are challenging other neighbourhoods. The idea is spreading. And don't think it's just the kids. Some of the adults are just as bad. And who do

you imagine is our team's coach? Wrong! It's Jim.
And who provides the refreshments? Marg. And who
sits on the pavement cheering her old head off? Well,
Myrtle does – when it's not too cold.

Yes, things have changed quite a lot since What's-
his-name moved in.

What would your neighbourhood look like if Jesus
moved in? And how would it affect Fred?

Meeting our neighbours

Our home in British Columbia was in an older,
established neighbourhood. We moved there because
we liked the house and because it was only a short
walk from my office. The objective of loving our
neighbours and seeing Jesus' presence expressed
through us – well, it simply never occurred to us. We
lived there a whole year before the challenge hit.

We were on the corner, where tall trees and high
fences established the neighbourhood as a private
place to live, the kind of environment where people
keep to themselves. The neighbours opposite lived in
a strange old shack back in the woods. It must have
been there since long before the land was subdivided
and houses were built. It was set in five acres of
undergrowth and trees. The garage was nearest the
road, moss-covered, decaying and decorated with an
animal skull nailed over the door. What we could see
of the house suggested that one good strong wind
could solve the problem. Of the occupants we saw
little. But we did hear them. They had loud parties

until late into the night and frequently we would be woken at three in the morning with the squealing of tyres as their guests left. Next day there would be beer cans in the driveway and spilling out into the road. To love our neighbours was not an attractive proposition.

An evangelist came to town and held a crusade. We were challenged to invite our friends to hear him preach. We telephoned a few people we knew. Some said yes, but most declined. At least we had satisfied our consciences. We had participated in evangelism. We had invited our friends.

But what of our neighbours? The effort of getting up, going out of the house, walking over the road, going up their driveway, past the garage and the skull, dodging the brambles and ringing their door bell, was too much. What if they had a dog? Our feet just would not take us! Then it hit us that they were not our feet, but Jesus' feet. We feared our feelings being hurt by a rebuff until we remembered that they were not our feelings, but Jesus' feelings. We feared embarrassing them by laying our religion on strangers, until we remembered that Jesus had given his whole body to be crucified to remove from them the embarrassment of sin. So Jesus' feet walked over the road and Jesus' finger rang the bell and Jesus' mouth delivered the invitation and Jesus' ears suffered the usual rebuff when they said that they were just not interested in religion.

But at least contact had been made. We knew their names and they ours. We resolved to pray for them. The next party they held, they invited us! 'Come on over and meet my brother,' said

Boomer. 'You'll be interested to meet him. He's religious too.' How badly we had misjudged them. There we had sat, in our splendid religious isolation. Boomer and Kim were the most delightful people, with a new baby called Ashley. Our daughter started to baby-sit for them. They let us keep our horse on their field. We kept their grass mowed when they went away on holiday. They helped our daughter when the horse got through the fence and laid a trail of hoofmarks over the neighbour's lawn en route to depositing fertiliser on the neighbour's roses. We helped them move some furniture. They let us cry on their shoulders when we were worried about our kids. There never were better neighbours than Boomer and Kim. We thought loving our neighbours would be something we would do to them, but they outdid us in love and kindness. We invited them to attend a religious meeting, but they invited us into their home! Did we represent Jesus to them or they to us?

Meet Brian and Dianne Dahl

Brian and Dianne Dahl, together with their two teenage children, Gordon and Katherine, moved west from Ontario in 1989. Brian had been brought up there and Dianne, being a Massachusetts girl, had always felt a bit of an outsider, immersed as she was in Brian's town, Brian's family, Brian's church. But when Brian and Dianne bought a house in Maple Ridge, British Columbia, it was a level playing field. Brian's father, Ralph, had been diagnosed with cancer and he and his wife Laura moved too, buying the show house next door to Brian and Dianne's new property.

So there they were in a new house in a new town in a new province. The church that had been home for the past twenty years was 4,000 kilometres away. They were surrounded by strangers. They felt like aliens. 'God, where do we fit? Where do we belong? What shall we do?'

When you are new and a long way from all that is familiar, mail becomes very important. But one day soon after they moved in the postman delivered nothing but junk mail. Only one item bore their name and that was hardly personal. It was a magazine published by a conference centre.

The leading article caught Brian's eye: 'I am not ashamed of the gospel . . . or am I?' it was headed, and was on how to introduce your neighbours to Jesus, written by yours truly. He read the article out loud to Dianne and gradually a picture formed in their minds of their new neighbourhood as a place where Jesus lived. Jesus himself would make it a place of friendship and caring, where people would not live in selfish isolation but would be good citizens, knowing each other and sharing what they had.

Meet Andy and Stephanie Peters

Andy and Stephanie Peters moved house from Vancouver to the suburb of Langley because of work. Andy is in banking and bankers have to go where the money is. Still, their home church was only 45 minutes away by car, so at least they would be able to continue to attend. Perhaps they could even establish a satellite group to care for the needs of other members who lived in Langley.

But it seemed the whole earth was without form, and void. Their house, set on one side of the bulge of the cul-de-sac, was the first house to be built in a new subdivision and it was surrounded by a sea of mud and excavators. Their little children were for ever tracking dirt into the house on to the brand-new carpet.

'What are we doing here?' crossed their minds more than once. So they started to pray for their not-yet-arrived neighbours. 'Please send us the right neighbours so we can love them, as you taught us to.'

Mandy and Vic moved in right next door. Mandy had just become a Christian a matter of weeks before making the move, so both she and the person who had introduced her to Jesus had been praying that there would be Christians in their new neighbourhood. There was one answer to everyone's prayer.

Jonathan and Melody were from a huge church in town. They were bakers and kept uncivilised hours. They moved in on the other side.

Trevor and Leah, together with their two boys, moved in on the opposite side of the cul-de-sac. It seemed Leah had been loosely involved with a church at some point in her past, but religion was now firmly on the back burner. Trevor was an atheist.

Frank and Lois were older than the other newcomers. They were Catholics, but hardly devout. Lois had at one time been a nun but had left the order in favour of marrying Frank. Their children had left home, so their nest felt a little empty. Frank, who had been quite an athlete in his younger years, now had a gammy leg and walked with a frustrating limp.

Sam and Pauline lived three doors down. They at least appeared to have no past church connections whatsoever.

Ted and Emma were not going to be easy. They were stand-offish and unfriendly. But their redeeming feature was their two little girls. Kids love company, so though the parents were reluctant to come out and play, Kimmy and Beverly soon made friends with Bob and Paul. 'Actually, I do have some religious connections,' Emma confided in Stephanie one day, over a cup of coffee. 'My grandparents became Baptists and insisted in dragging me along. They hadn't always been religious, but when they were around retirement age they got into it in a big way, and I was the one who suffered for it! I suppose they thought they would have to make up for lost time!'

'God, please do something special in this neighbourhood, something bigger and better than we could ever think to ask.' Andy and Stephanie prayed for all their new neighbours.

One day when Andy had gone off to work, the boys were watching *Sesame Street* and the baby had been fed, Stephanie was enjoying a cup of coffee while she read her Bible and prayed for the neighbourhood. As she prayed a picture formed in her mind. There was the cul-de-sac with all the new houses around it. And there, right in the middle of the circle, stood Jesus. He stood tall, higher than the street lights. She seemed to hear a voice say: 'Jesus is big in this neighbourhood.' So strong was the impression that Stephanie laughed out loud, and went on chuckling to herself all day at the thought of Jesus being big in her neighbourhood.

How could Jesus become big in your neighbourhood?

6

Taking the Initiative

Kindness in Jesus' name makes his friendship known

Whatever you do, whether in word or deed, do it all in the name of the Lord Jesus, giving thanks. . .

Anyone who gives . . . a cup of water in my name . . . will certainly not lose his reward.

One of the most compelling aspects of the introduction of our friends to Jesus is the love expressed through the Church at large. In virtually every corner of the globe there are members of the body of Jesus taking the initiative to express his kindness to people in need. There are health clinics, hospitals, schools, orphanages, agricultural training programmes and the like, all offering practical, tangible evidence of the loving reality of Jesus. This is more than a handshake, more than a hug, more than a shoulder to cry on. This is the kind of love you can grab hold of and climb on to.

'Is Jesus real? Or is he just a distant divinity one can seek comfort from by holding imaginary conversations with him?'

'No! Come and see what he did for my village. See the school he started. He still touches lepers and heals blind eyes . . .'

And you don't have to travel overseas to see overwhelming evidence of the touch of Jesus through his body. Right in the community where I live there is an open door to single mothers, offering free day-care, advice, practical help with such matters as employment and constant friendship. In our town the young people who hang around the shopping centre, the youth gangs, the teenage runaways, have three doors that I am aware of open to them, offering friendship and all the practical support they could dream of. The very best deals in town are offered by a free store at one church. They offer clothes, baby equipment and household goods to any who are in need. As it's a border town, there is a steady flow of refugees from central America. The church has a team of translators and legal advisors to help them into the country. Then they offer a network of people who give them accommodation and help them find work.

As an individual I can no more address all these needs than my elbow can listen to a symphony! But I am part of a wonderful body, and despite its spots and wrinkles I am proud of it because it is Jesus' body.

But Fred is not a refugee, a single mother or a runaway teenager and so has never had to take

advantage of any of the wonderful facilities offered
by the church in our town. And because of the wonderful Canadian health service, Fred is unaware of
Christian-run hospitals. In his mind, Grace Hospital
in Vancouver derives its name from some female
benefactor rather than from the Salvation Army's
understanding of the grace of God. And Fred makes
no connection between St Paul's Hospital and the
man who wrote half the New Testament. These are
state-run facilities, and the fact that the whole world
is littered with wonderful institutions inspired by the
love of Jesus does almost nothing to touch Fred.

Kindness to a neighbour is cheaper than becoming a missionary

Recently I worked with a church in Vancouver. It
was a mission weekend and the pastor told me that
the emphasis in previous years had been on the work
being done overseas. The call had been to the three
young people at the back of the gallery to 'Go into all
the world . . .' and for the rest to put an extra note in
the offering basket. On Sunday morning I preached
from the pulpit about the prime missionary call being
to love your neighbour. 'There is little value in going
overseas to express the love of Jesus until you have
done the same for your neighbours.'

In the evening I offered them practical training
in how to introduce a friend to Jesus. I suggested
that they should recognise that the church was Jesus
in that neighbourhood. 'What difference would he
make if he lived right here, on this corner? What

would people ask of him if they met him in the street, at the bus stop, over the fence?'

Monday morning was a holiday and I invited everyone to come with me to express the love of Jesus to the immediate neighbours of the church. A few timid souls arrived at 9.30 in the morning, and following prayer we went out two by two. 'Now remember,' I primed them. 'Two of you going in Jesus' name represents his presence. Ask the people you meet what they want him to do for them, for their family, for this neighbourhood.' In the forty-five years of the church's life, this had never been done.

I started out with the pastor of the church, who was as nervous as anyone else. We visited three houses, then he had to rush off to visit a member in the hospital. So I was alone, with Jesus.

Opposite me I could see another couple visiting the houses on the other side of the street. They were raking leaves! I crossed to find out what they were playing at. An elderly lady had opened the door, and when asked what she wanted God to do for her she suggested that, as God had supposedly made the leaves on her trees, then he might have the decency to rake them up when they fell on her lawn. So, very wisely, instead of praying that God would send a great wind, they asked for rakes and set to work. Jesus was raking up the leaves!

I went back to my side of the street and found a lady raking the leaves from her lawn. I imagine the coincidence of a rainless day in November with a holiday is sufficiently rare to make leaf-raking the highest priority of the day.

'Excuse me!' It doesn't take much of an excuse to stop a person raking leaves. 'I'm representing the church at the top of the street. We are praying for this neighbourhood and would like to know what other people around us are wanting God to do for this community. What do you want God to do for the people in this street?'

She leaned on the rake. 'Asians. They seem to be so isolated. I would like God to do something to break down the barriers that separate us.'

'I can agree wholeheartedly. Could we pray one sentence together to ask God to do just that?'

'OK,' she agreed. So I led off in a brief prayer.

The very next house I called at was an Asian home. A lady with white hair and brown wrinkled skin came timidly to the door and stuck her head out.

'I'm representing the church at the top of the street. We are praying specially for our neighbourhood and are wondering what others are wanting God to do for us all. What do you want God to do for this community?'

'Well, it's not a very friendly community. I have lived here for five years and I don't know any of the neighbours.' That certainly married up with the previous prayer request.

'Is there anything particular that you personally want God's help with, or something for the family, perhaps?'

Her eyes misted up. 'My husband has left me with my three sons and has gone back to India leaving us with no financial support. Can your God do anything about that?'

'He most certainly can!' I boasted.

Then she broke down and wept. 'There's more,' she wailed. 'My daughter-in-law Tina has lived here these past four years and I have virtually raised her little girl, Amman. Six weeks ago she upped and left and I don't knew where she is or what to do and I miss her so much.' I wept too. I'm soft that way. But if someone did that to my grandchildren I'd weep. And someone had done it to a little child and to an elderly lady that Jesus loved, so he wept through my eyes.

Together we prayed on her doorstep in Jesus' name for Amman and Tina and the husband.

Now I couldn't take a rake and address the problem as had the folk over the road. There was no way I could find Tina, and even if I could I doubt I could have persuaded her to go home. But I could pray, and I could do something else. I was part of a body, connected to others who were better qualified to help. When I got back to the church I reported what had happened.

'I know just the person to help!' exclaimed the pastor. He got right on the telephone to a retired missionary couple who had served in India and spoke the lady's language. They lit up with the joy of being able to do something to help and went right over to meet her. They got her in touch with a local Punjabi fellowship.

Writing this paragraph has prompted me to phone the church to find out if Amman and her mother are still away. I suppose I should not have been surprised to learn that Amman is back with her grandmother, though Tina, her mother, is still absent. It seems that our prayer was answered. I asked the pastor about the lady whose leaves were raked. 'Last week I took her tea and biscuits and a copy of the "Daily Bread" Bible-reading notes. She is very friendly and welcomes my visits. But she is not yet open to coming to church.'

It's hard to love your neighbour if you don't even know his name

Being the newcomers on the block in an established neighbourhood can make it difficult to make friends. So when we were faced with the challenge of inviting our new neighbours to attend an evangelistic crusade, we hardly knew where to begin. We quickly concluded that we had missed the bus as far as this opportunity was concerned. However, we determined to put things right.

There had been some break-ins in the neighbourhood and people were nervous about locking their doors. So were we. Then an inspiration struck us.

We contacted the local police station and asked if it would be possible for an officer to come to our neighbourhood to talk to us all about security. They readily agreed and we made a plan for the following Friday evening. Then we set out to visit all our neighbours. 'Hi,' we introduced ourselves. 'We are Justyn and Joy and are new to the neighbourhood. We have taken over the house on the corner. We heard there have been some house break-ins, and being nervous we went to the police who have promised to send an officer to come to give us some guidance on how to make our homes safer.

Of course, it also makes a great excuse for us to get to know our new neighbours. So would you come? Next Friday at 8.00.' Most readily agreed, though some had other plans.

We took the names and phone numbers of everyone, made a map of the thirty homes that constituted our neighbourhood and handed out a copy to everyone so we would all be better equipped to watch each other's backs. Now we knew everybody by name. But the evening with the police started to build friendship. Joy is a wonderful cook and provided mouth-watering, heart-warming, ice-breaking treats. Everyone wanted to know what we did for a living. The news that I was a preacher was a bit of a downer, but the fact that I did not preach that evening was a universal relief.

Boomer and Kim were there, all smiles. Bob and Helen from next door were so glad to meet their new neighbours. The previous couple who had lived in our house had split up and had been rather unfriendly.

Mabel Childs was the oldest inhabitant. She was a retired school teacher, widely read and interested in many subjects. She seldom went out and never tended her garden. Having lived there for thirty years, she had seen people come and go from the neighbourhood and now didn't trouble to get to know her neighbours, all of whom she considered to be transients. But she was pleased with the idea of neighbours caring for each other and keeping an eye open for thieves.

Thus we struck a blow against the enemy of unneighbourliness! The whole neighbourhood now knew each other's names and were keeping an eye on each other's properties. Jesus had said: 'You shall not steal,' and in his name we were doing our best to banish such unneighbourly behaviour from our street.

Taking the initiative in friendship

Andy and Stephanie Peters had the advantage of being the first in a brand-new section of houses. As each new house was completed, the new occupants would be greeted by a warm welcome and sometimes some sandwiches or even a pie to help overcome the trauma of moving day. One by one the Peters made friends with their new neighbours. 'We had no agenda, no technique that we were following, no tracts hidden in the sandwiches. We just knew that Jesus was big in our neighbourhood, and so we acted as he would have done.'

Once there were enough neighbours to constitute a neighbourhood, they would organise pot-luck suppers to welcome newcomers. Though this started in their own home, they quickly passed on the responsibility of actually being the hosts, so that others could enjoy the privilege of taking Jesus' role of host to the neighbourhood. Of course, not everybody understood it in those terms, for Andy and Stephanie never spoke of it like that.

Steph was a basketball enthusiast. She loved the game. Working with teenagers had been her thing back in their home church, but few teenagers moved into their cul-de-sac. Undaunted, she determined to keep the whole neighbourhood fit – in Jesus' name, of course! Steph persuaded half a dozen neighbours to provide some funds to purchase two hoops and stands, then organised the men into sinking them in the ground, one in their own front garden and the other on the opposite side of the cul-de-sac bulge, on the edge of Trevor and Leah's plot. Soon everyone was out playing, kids and adults. 'Neighbours that play together, stay together' is an old adage that Confucius ought to have thought of, for it's true.

Stephanie would go over to Frank and Lois's house; remember? – the older couple. 'Can Frank come out and play?' she would ask! And out he would come, hopping and limping around the cul-de-sac on his wrecked knee. This was undoubtedly the most fun neighbourhood he had ever lived in!

October presented the prospect of children threatening the neighbourhood with tricks if treats were not forthcoming. 'Jesus is big in this neighbourhood,' they thought. 'What would he do?'

It was Jonathan and Melody who came up with the idea of a neighbourhood Hallowe'en street party. So, down-playing the unpleasant images and encouraging the fun, Andy and Stephanie joined Jonathan and Melody in hosting the best Hallowe'en that anyone could remember. A Hallowe'en street party in that neighbourhood is now a firmly established tradition.

Andy and Stephanie don't see their activities as friendship evangelism, for that would imply a hidden agenda. They see themselves as Jesus' agents for friendship in their neighbourhood, and in his name they take the initiative to see that everyone who lives there knows and likes each other. 'Love your neighbour' is their mandate and they take it literally. What started as obedience to a command has become natural. For spending time and doing things with good friends is hardly an irksome duty. And the strangers whom they obediently loved as neighbours are now their friends whom they love from the heart.

The neighbourhood street party

Brian and Dianne Dahl saw their new neighbourhood in much the same way. There was a whole street of houses, and they were determined that the reality of Jesus would make that a special place to live. Like us, they soon realised that you cannot love your neighbour if you don't even know his name.

So one evening Brian, in company with his thirteen-year-old daughter Katherine, set out to survey the street. 'Hi, I'm Brian and this is my daughter Katherine. We live just up the street. We are new to the neighbourhood and thought it might be a great idea if we held a neighbourhood barbecue, a street party. That way we could all get better acquainted. What do you think?'

Without exception everyone thought it was a wonderful idea; only one family would not be able to make it on the Monday of the next holiday weekend, and that was because they would be away on holiday.

Brian used his research to create a neighbourhood directory which he gave to everyone so names would no longer be a barrier to neighbourliness. Along with the directory he gave a proper invitation to the street party, to be held at 5.00 p.m. on the holiday Monday.

Everyone agreed to bring something. Antonio and Marie brought a huge bowl of home-made pasta.

'I'll bring a few cases of beer,' someone offered.

'Great,' Brian wisely responded, 'but just be sensitive to the kids who will be there. It's a family event.'

'Why are you doing this?' asked another neighbour suspiciously.

'Just to get to know the neighbours.'

'No other agenda?' Again he probed.

'Why do you ask?'

'Well, I see you folks going out to church every Sunday morning, so I assume you are Christians.'

'Yes, we are.'

'Well, so am I! My name's Sam. Is there anything I can do to help?'

'Since you ask, there is,' said Brian, relieved. 'Just before we eat, when introductions have been made, would you pray a one-sentence grace? Please don't make it a sermon, just "Thank you, Father, for this food and this friendly neighbourhood. In Jesus' name."' Sam readily agreed.

The day dawned cloudy. It had rained all weekend, but the forecast was for clearing skies that afternoon. At the appointed hour they all came, twenty-seven households of neighbours. Even the family who had declined the invitation cut short their holiday because they were determined not to miss the fun. Some were a little nervous, but all were in agreement that this was good. It is right to be good neighbours.

Brian is a great organiser. He got everyone to stand in two lines facing each other, each family in position representing where they lived up the street. Then they introduced themselves, household by household. Nobody minded and everyone appreciated the exercise of getting to know the other neighbours.

One set of neighbours had been eyeing another with that terrible feeling that they ought to know each other, but weren't quite sure how. But as soon as names and introductions had been made they recognised each other as former neighbours. They had lived right next door to each other for six years in another town, but had never actually met until then. Another couple recognised each other from their days together at school fifteen years previously.

Sam did a great job saying grace. God heard it and it seemed that everyone else thought it was 'nice' as they listened in.

The atmosphere in the street was never the same after that. They were a neighbourhood where people talked to each other, knew each other's names, liked each other. Jesus was doing his thing, and unlike religion, his thing was right up everyone's street.

7

Establishing the Rendezvous

Meeting in Jesus' name defines where he can be found

Where two or three come together in my name, there am I with them.

If 'omnipresent' had been a part of King David's vocabulary, he would have used it in Psalm 139, but sadly theologians did not think it up until years later. But he did know that God was everywhere. There was no escaping God, in the depths of the sea, in the heights of the heavens, in the remotest corners of the earth, even in a mother's womb. God's presence was everywhere, all at the same time.

So in the neighbourhood he is out in the cul-de-sac, in the alley behind the houses, on the lawn, by the post box – everywhere, all at once.

I daresay Fred might be a little less familiar with

the concept of 'omnipresent' than was David, even if he could spell it. 'Hey, Fred, where is God?' He might make gestures towards the sky and mutter something about 'somebody up there'. He might point to the church building down the way. It would be unlikely to occur to him that God was as close as breathing.

In a neighbourhood it makes things a whole lot simpler if Jesus has an address somewhere, some house, some place where someone looking to find him can easily do so. That is where the event of 'two of three coming together in his name' becomes useful. Jesus promised '*there* am I with them'. Of course he is everywhere, but everywhere is . . . well, it's nowhere in particular. And of course he is present in the local church building, but that is not part of the immediate neighbourhood and is a little scary and inaccessible to people who never go. But supposing a few neighbours got together over a cup of coffee in one of the houses round the cul-de-sac to pursue Jesus' agenda. Who would show up in a very special way? The one whose name would be proclaimed by the two or three meeting in that name. Jesus.

A specific address at a specific time

Roger was not your average church pew-stuffer. He grew up in Manchester and emigrated to Canada some years back. He worked as an engineer for a big brewery in Vancouver. I always liked Roger for his frank way of speaking and for his caring attitude towards the people around him. Anyway, he used to come and listen to me preach from time to time, and I always like people who do that.

One day, at the end of one of my sermons, he said: 'Justyn, as far as I can see Jesus never claimed to be the Son of God. That's something men have tacked on since, much like the legends of Robin Hood.'

'That's baloney, Roger. He made it very clear who he was. In fact the whole reason he got crucified was because of his refusal to back down from exactly that claim.' And I showed him it all in the Bible.

'Well, bloody hell!' says Roger. (I don't think he read that in the Bible.) 'I never knew that before.'

'Why don't you come and join our fellowship group that meets on a Wednesday night? We study the Bible.'

'No bloody fear! You wouldn't catch me at a Bible study! And anyway, who would look after the kids? I can't afford a sitter.'

'Then why don't we meet in your home? You invite some of your friends and neighbours and so will I. That way we'd all be starting from scratch.'

Roger warmed to the idea. His wife Patsy laid on wonderful goodies and we started to meet every Thursday evening. Roger and Patsy only lived a couple of streets away, so we invited Boomer and Kim, our neighbours from across the road. Remembering their blunt refusal to accept the invitation we had given them to attend the evangelistic crusade, we anticipated another snub.

'Hey, that sounds like a good idea! Just a group of people getting together to discuss issues related to parenting, being good neighbours, making marriage work, that kind of stuff?'

'Yes, that's what we had in mind. We will base the discussions on the Bible and will pray about some of the things which come up.'

'Can't do us any harm! Count us in. What time does it start?'

Bill and Lynn Dealey, who lived opposite 'the Christians', came too. It was now their car that crowded the driveway and impeded the street hockey! Ah well, what goes around, comes around.

Roger and Patsy pulled in a couple of neighbours and we were away.

Carol phoned me the following week. She made it clear that she was not a Christian but wanted to know more. Next week she joined the group. 'This is just what I need,' she announced over coffee. 'I'm not ready for church. But I want to find out what God is all about without being forced to join anything. I am very interested in God, but I must confess to being less than interested in church and religion.'

Over the weeks that followed there were several people I encountered to whom I gave an invitation to come along to a specific address at a definite time. And there they met the person in whose name we all met, the one whose presence became increasingly apparent as we pursued his agenda.

An event to launch a series

Dear Justyn,
 We are trying to form a neighbourhood Bible

study, and we understand that you have some experience in this. Would you be willing to come to help us get started, perhaps speak at the first meeting . . . ?

Right up my street! But I phoned back. 'How many of your neighbours are the kind of people who are into Bible study?'

'There are two Christian families on our street, but we really wanted to do something that would attract the neighbours who are not Christians.'

'Do you know your neighbours?'

'Oh yes! This is a very friendly neighbourhood. We often have barbecues together. The kids all go to the same school and so we mothers all know each other.'

'Well, how about starting out with an event that may be a little less daunting to someone who thinks that Genesis is in the same Testament as Nintendo?'

'What would you suggest?'

'How about inviting your neighbours to a neighbourhood pot-luck supper and tell them that the evening will include a discussion on the theme of "How to make this neighbourhood a happier, safer, better place to live"?'

'We thought that a series of meetings would be best, not just a one-off event.'

'Yes, but an open-ended commitment to meet every Wednesday evening for the rest of their lives to discuss the Bible . . . ? Isn't that a bit hard to swallow? What I am suggesting is an event from which a regular meeting might be born.'

They took a day or so to think the idea over, then called back enthusiastically.

'You're on! But we slightly changed the title so that it wouldn't imply that this neighbourhood is not already a good place to live in. And we also wanted to make it clear that there would be a Christian agenda.'

The invitations went out and the people came, intrigued by the idea of a discussion on 'How to make this neighbourhood an even happier, safer, better place to live in, with God's help'.

I arrived early so that I could meet the hosts before their guests arrived. The gathering was in a townhouse, part of a complex of homes clustered around a central courtyard. Little wonder the hosts knew every one of their neighbours, and it occurred to me that they would have to live with them after this evening was all over!

Tom and Joanne were a couple in their mid-thirties. They obviously had children, but there was no sign of them. 'The kids are out for a sleep-over with a friend,' Joanne explained. Tom was a mechanic and his wife was taking a few years out from the work force so as to concentrate on the children. 'This is Ed and Janet from across the way. It's OK, they are believers' – as though it would not have been OK had they not been!

I took it that Ed was a long-established Christian. 'I thought I would lead off in a prayer before you speak,' he told me. 'And I've brought along my guitar so we can sing a few worship songs to help people relax.'

'Don't you know any rugby songs?' I countered.

To Ed it was anathema to start a Christian meeting without a prayer and some singing. I'm not sure that I convinced him, but at least I secured his agreement that he would leave his guitar in its box, and that while we would pray together now before the other neighbours arrived, we would not embarrass people who were not used to praying once the guests arrived.

'Who are you expecting?' I asked them all.

'Well, just about everyone I asked is coming,' Joanne jumped in eagerly, anxious (I think) to steer the conversation away from opening prayers and guitars. 'Most of them never go to church as far as we can see. The couple three doors down are Catholic but seem a bit suspicious of us charismatic Protestants. The lady next door is coming. She is heavily into New Age, in fact she has a steady stream of people coming to her for readings or counsel or whatever they do. I'm sure she will have plenty to say.'

We prayed together for the evening, briefly because Joanne was busy with last-minute preparations. 'Tom, mix the punch now!' she commanded from the kitchen. Ed went white. 'Punch!' he echoed. 'Not alcoholic, I hope! But what happens if someone brings a bottle of wine?'

'Then take a little wine for your neighbour's sake,' I misquoted the Scripture, with some justification. After all, the cause of loving a neighbour was rather more worthy than fixing a wobbly stomach.

'But I never touch the stuff.'

'And neither do many people who are not Christians. So why make an issue over it? You don't have to drink it, but if it helps your neighbours to feel more at home by permitting them to do something that Jesus himself clearly did with his neighbours, then why spoil the party over it?'

The evening was a great success. Forty-five people must have been there, jammed into that living-room on that dark rainy night. And Joanne was right. It was a very friendly neighbourhood. Ed's worst fears were realised. Two or three bottles arrived, and a couple of six-packs. Tom graciously accepted them and they went on the sideboard along with the punch. People chose their own poison without embarrassment and without feeling that anyone was disapproving of their social habits.

The New Age lady was in her thirties, thin as a stick with a pinched face and needle-sharp eyes. Put a pointed black hat on her head and a broomstick in her hand and she'd have been all set for Hallowe'en! Doreen, her name was, and she never relaxed.

When everyone was well into the ambience of neighbourliness, Tom called the gathering to order and managed to get most people seated, some on chairs, some on arms, some on the floor and some up the stairs.

I was terrified that Ed would leap in with a rousing chorus of 'Rescue the Perishing', but happily he was silent. 'I want to introduce you to our good friend, Justyn Rees. He lives in Mount Lehman and heads a team of concerned citizens on a cross-Canada trek with a theme of reconciliation – bringing together our wrecked and silly nation! He is of the opinion that reconciliation starts in the heart and is then expressed through home and neighbourhood. The politicians' approach starts in Ottawa and is imposed from the top through legislation. So we asked Justyn to come and share with us some thoughts on how our neighbourhood can be part of the solution rather than part of the problem. Justyn, tell us: how can we make this neighbourhood an even better place to live?'

I won't weary you by repeating all I had to say, but I will assure you that I was all done in ten minutes. I finished by taking a leaf out of my own book, which I had not yet written . . .

'We are convinced that God is not just interested in religion, but in every aspect of the life of our country and community. We have been going door to door in each community we have visited across Canada to ask people what they are wanting God to do for Canada, for that particular community and for themselves personally. So why don't we do the same thing here tonight? Let's start by sharing our requests for our country. If you could ask God for one thing to make Canada a better place to live, what would you ask for?'

This was relatively impersonal and people freely shared their wish list. It also served to open us all up to each other. At one point it came close to a political argument, but it was all in good humour. Nearer to home someone was concerned about the rising number of houses that had been broken into during the daytime. Someone else wanted more play areas for the children. Ed wanted the Lord's Prayer back in schools.

Then I made it more personal: 'If God said to you: "What do you want me to do for you personally, or for your family?", what would you ask?'

This line of thinking avoided arguments about differing views of religion and homed in on matters that were close to the heart of each person present. Certainly, there is a time and place for religious debate, but this was not it. It was a group of neighbours who had met in friendship, not to argue over religion but to think about how they might improve their neighbourhood.

I shared my request first, to help get things rolling. The Catholic couple were very concerned for their teenage daughter who was not doing well at school and was getting into the wrong company. When it came to Doreen, the New Age lady, I wondered what to expect. However, something about being faced with the idea of standing before God with the opportunity for one request cut through the superficial wrapping of her life and reached her heart.

'If I could ask God for one thing,' she started out bravely, 'I would ask him for forgiveness.' Then she choked. Through her sobs she kept saying: 'Forgiveness. Forgiveness. That is what I want. I know about it, but I can't experience it.'

Ed and Janet, who were sitting right next to her, immediately put their arms round her and quietly encouraged her towards the only one who could possibly grant that request. For who on earth has power to forgive sins but Jesus?

While they were quietly continuing in a corner, I concluded the discussion by introducing the idea of a regular weekly meeting for neighbours. 'I am not proposing a church meeting or a heavy discussion.

Just a time when in friendship you who live here can pursue the agenda of making this an even better place to live. I suggest you use the Bible as a resource book. It is an all-time worldwide best seller and is the universally accepted classic textbook on loving your neighbour. You could take a few paragraphs each week and discuss together how that teaching might affect this neighbourhood and your family, for good. You might also take time to pray specifically for any issues that seem relevant at the time, even praying for requests phoned in by other neighbours who might not have the time to attend themselves. Then you could discuss positive action that you might take together, a special event that could be planned, some recreational facilities that you might want to purchase together.' I told them about Andy and Stephanie's basketball hoops.

The relevance of what I was proposing, together with the practical benefit of it, was not lost on anyone. This was not religion, but good neigh-bourliness.

'How many would be interested in such a gathering?' asked Tom. Several raised tentative fingers, and they were launched. The following week eight people came, and the last I heard they are still meeting. Anyone in that complex of houses who wants to know where they can meet with Jesus knows exactly where and when they can do so. It doesn't always happen in the same home, but it is always in the neighbourhood. Jesus belongs to the neighbourhood, not to a church up the road. He lives there.

Using a family crisis to introduce Jesus to the neighbourhood

Ralph Dahl died of cancer three years after he and Laura had moved into the same neighbourhood as their son and daughter-in-law, Brian and Dianne. His passing was unremarkable except to those who knew him best. A couple of months before, Laura had released him to the Lord Jesus, finding peace in her heart through the confidence that her heavenly Father loved Ralph even more than she did. 'I want you fellows to do the same,' Ralph told his sons, Brian and Dave. 'It's no good struggling to keep me here. God knows what's best for all of us. But I want you to pray that I won't suffer at the end.'

And Ralph didn't suffer. Over the few days which followed, his body just closed down. He slipped into unconsciousness from which he never awoke, in that neighbourhood at least.

The very next day Brian printed a notice telling his neighbours that his father, their neighbour, had died and giving thanks to God for his life and the manner of his death. He invited them all to attend the memorial service that would be held the following Monday evening in the Baptist church.

It says much for how highly the Dahl family were regarded in that neighbourhood that seventeen neighbours came. The pastor delivered a fine message giving praise to God for the gospel (which he carefully explained), a gospel which had given Ralph a wonderful way to live and a positive way to die. Both Brian and his brother Dave also spoke.

Several neighbours were very moved. 'We heard things tonight that we have never in our lives heard before,' said Graham and Heidi from next door. 'We have some hard thinking to do.'

Wayne, a retired police chief, was accustomed to death. 'But your dad was special,' he told Brian. 'Within twenty minutes of meeting him I was sharing with him things I wouldn't even tell my wife! He certainly knew how to live and it seems now that he also knew how to die. We have to talk!'

Ralph's 'unremarkable' death was a matter of great remark in his neighbourhood. A neighbour had died in the neighbourhood and had done it in style. There was something different about it that people just couldn't leave alone. Why did the Dahls react so differently? What was it about them?

So when Brian and Dianne proposed a regular meeting for neighbours in their home, half a dozen neighbours readily agreed. 'We will be discussing normal matters of life and death in the light of what the Bible teaches,' they were told. And so, arising out of death, came life. A new group of neighbours started to pursue the agenda of the one in whose name they met, an invisible neighbour whose presence became increasingly obvious with each meeting.

A church fellowship group evolves into a neighbourhood group

When Andy and Stephanie moved into their new

home they had high hopes of establishing a satellite for their large city church, Kingsway Chapel. Within ten minutes' drive of them were several members of that church, all eager for midweek fellowship while anxious to avoid another commute into the centre of the city.

Jonathan and Melody next door were from Dunbar Christian Fellowship, another flourishing city church, and gratefully joined the Kingsway Chapel adherents for similar reasons. Mandy was brand new and had no denominational preferences. So they established a regular meeting in their home, as an uneasy mix of members of Kingsway Chapel who lived in the area and neighbours who lived next door.

And an uneasy mix it was. Kingsway Chapel was well organised. The pastor produced discussion material each week which keyed into his Sunday morning sermon. These carefully prepared questions formed the basis for discussion at the weekly meeting in Andy and Stephanie's home. Water and oil don't mix, and a church syllabus and a neighbourhood agenda sometimes have similar problems.

'Are we missing something?' someone from the neighbourhood would ask. 'Are we meant to know something about tithing?' Well, yes, they would know all about it had they listened to the pastor's sermon the previous Sunday morning in Kingsway Chapel. 'And what's this about missions emphasis week? Are we planning to send missionaries from here?'

'The Elders feel it is important to keep all the Bible study groups following the same syllabus each week,' explained the director of Christian education at Kingsway Chapel. 'That way we will all be moving along together as a fellowship.'

It took a couple of years but eventually, and with reluctance, Andy and Stephanie checked out a local church. It was brand new and meeting in a nearby primary school. The pastor was delighted to see a whole family of mature Christians headed his way, but Andy and Stephanie wisely fielded all the opportunities for joining the church council or teaching in Sunday School. 'We just want to concentrate all our efforts on our neighbourhood, loving our neighbours as our main area of Christian service. We don't want to get so involved in the good things that are happening in this church that we will have no time or energy left over for our neighbours.' The pastor was thrilled, and not only gave them his blessing but promised to pray for them.

And so it was that the Kingsway Chapel Bible study group evolved into a neighbourhood support group. As soon as the agenda switched to the neighbourhood, other neighbours joined. They had seen little point in attending a meeting built around the agenda of a church in town, but a meeting of neighbours for neighbours was a different matter.

Cars parking in the driveway and spilling out on to the street were no problem. It was neighbours who came, and most of them walked. And in any case, the basketball would not be disturbed by 'the Christians' for all the people in the meeting were the noisy basketball players. Perhaps other neighbours might get at least one evening of peace and quiet each week!

There was a new resident with an address in the neighbourhood. He had made his presence felt through friendly action and now his presence was represented by neighbours meeting in his name to pursue his agenda. For where two or three come together in his name, inevitably Jesus shows up in person.

8

Laying the Red Carpet

Welcoming others in Jesus' name makes him accessible

Jesus took a little child and had him stand among them. Taking him in his arms, he said to them, 'Whoever welcomes one of these little children in my name welcomes me; and whoever welcomes me does not welcome me but the one who sent me.'

Welcome one another, then, just as Christ welcomed you, in order to bring praise to God.

I am seldom as vulnerable as when meeting new people. What if they don't like me? What if they ignore me, fail to laugh at my humour, think I'm stupid? What if I behave inappropriately for their culture, make a social faux pas or two?

Oh the relief when the introduction has been made and I am accepted. They smile, listen to what I have to say, introduce me to their friends. I am welcome.

Cheers! The place where everybody knows my name. I am in!

Wal-Mart, so big that nobody could possibly know my name! But the very successful directors of that huge North American chain of department stores know that the first step to helping their customers part with their hard-earned cash is a welcome. 'Welcome to our Wal-Mart!' smiles the blue-jacketed greeter at the door. I know perfectly well that they aren't really pleased to see me. They are paid to say that hundreds of times each day. But it still works. A friendly smile and word of welcome boosts my confidence and I relax slightly and pull out my credit card.

Wal-Mart didn't invent greeters. Greeters have stood at the doors of churches for centuries. But I sometimes wonder if they don't take their job too seriously as they pin a small red flower to my lapel and give me a visitor's information pack. I feel conspicuous and out of place as it is, so why would I want to label myself as 'Visitor'? Then, to compound my chagrin, the pastor asks all visitors to get to their feet in front of the whole congregation. I tell my name and where I come from and am applauded. Do I feel welcome? Or do I feel even more self-conscious?

Some people have a definite gift as a welcomer. Albert Dobson was one such. Every Sunday morning he would be manning the door of St Nicholas' Church in Sevenoaks. Inevitably we were late. Getting three small children scrubbed, dressed and breakfasted on a Sunday morning seemed more difficult than it was on any other day of the week. So the first hymn and prayers would always be history by the time we arrived. But Albert never seemed to mind. There he was, opening the door and smiling. Somehow he made us all feel that we had done the church a tremendous honour just by coming. We were not late-comers, we were VIPs. He made us feel like Jesus himself. Yet it was Albert who was like Jesus, for he welcomed us in Jesus' name.

Turning rejection to a welcome

Moving into a new neighbourhood is not always easy. A few years back we moved from the town of White Rock to a more rural setting. The twenty-five houses that comprised our new neighbourhood were not clustered tightly round a cul-de-sac, but were strung out along a road a kilometre long. But we were still newcomers, townies who had invaded the countryside.

Our new home was a twenty-acre parcel of trees and brambles and a huge chicken barn with a broken back. I thought with great respect of the early pioneers with their axes and horse-drawn ploughs. But a bulldozer seemed more practical, so I bought a very old one. As it was being unloaded from the truck that delivered it I asked the driver: 'I have never driven one of these things. I am happy to discover how it works, but just tell me one vital thing. How do I stop it?' I drove it over the land to the dilapidated barn where I intended to store it. As I drove in through the door I realised at the last minute that the roll bar was higher than the lintel of the door. Panic erased from my mind the only bulldozer-driving lesson I had ever received. I did eventually stop it, but not until I had pulled the side of the barn in with me. Townies! No respect for the countryside!

Then there was the old pot-bellied cedar, a beautiful tree that had been a landmark there since anyone could remember. The trouble was that the tree had thoughtlessly taken root some centuries earlier right in the middle of the most convenient route for my future driveway. The cost of re-routing was likely to run to thousands, so with the aid of my trusty bulldozer the problem was solved ten minutes later. I was wrong! I admit it. One of my neighbours was so angry that she threatened to shoot me, not to kill but just to maim! We were not off to a good start!

A few doors up the road another newcomer was busy clearing his five acres of bluff property. He was a helicopter pilot, and trees and helicopters don't coexist peacefully. Jean purchased an even bigger bulldozer than mine, a huge old tank with a blade big enough to demolish half a forest at one pass. All the trees went. He re-routed the stream that had for centuries compliantly run through the site of his future helicopter-sized barn. He fed it into the ditch. All was well until the next heavy rain, then the ditch overflowed and filled his neighbour's basement. Townies!

But that wasn't the end of it. The driveway leading to his beautiful new house was built right on the lip of the steep bank which swept down several hundred feet to the river below. Steep banks that are held together by the roots of big trees will stay firm for centuries; remove those trees and that same bank will become a landslide. But Jean was a townie, so how would he know that, unless he learned the hard way? Next winter he learned. His drive disappeared, almost taking his barn with it. It was a good thing he had a helicopter. How else was he to get in and out of his property? Jean was not welcome in the neighbourhood and neither were we.

Joy and I took a trip to England to visit family and friends. Becky, our youngest, was away on a mission trip in Africa and our other two were adults, so we left them in charge of the property. For some reason our son Dan decided to throw a barbecue for a dozen of his friends. Word got out that *the* party was happening on a farm right out in the middle of nowhere. One lad even took it upon himself to photocopy a map of how to find our place. On one Saturday night in August five hundred youngsters arrived in cars and on motor bikes. Fires sprang up all over the field, beer flowed freely, fights broke out, neighbours complained – one even came out with a gun and fired shots into the air. The police came and the party was over. Semi-inebriated youngsters roared off up the road, shouting and hooting and taking detours over neighbours' lawns, leaving a trail of beer cans and broken bottles behind them.

Next day the media got wind of the party and our neighbourhood was news for miles around.

However, it was not international news. So, a week later, we arrived home from England in blissful ignorance of what had happened. It soon became apparent that we were not very welcome in our new neighbourhood. We received an anonymous letter, clearly from a neighbour, letting us know how deeply offended he was. It was just plain wrong that townies like us should move into the quietness of the country and bring all our noise and carry-on with us! The neighbourhood would not stand for it and we should not anticipate such a tolerant attitude towards us in the future. There would be ways of dealing with people like us!

Oh, it's great to be welcome, to be popular, to be in, part of the neighbourhood!

We held a family conference. Dan was terribly sorry. He had never intended it to be like that. He had only invited his close friends for a quiet barbecue. Yet we as a family were clearly responsible. What could we do? So we wrote a letter which we all signed, giving a copy to each neighbour. We apologised, ate humble pie, accepted responsibility, assured everyone that it would never happen again. And then the welcome came.

It was Jean who expressed it most eloquently. He wrote us a lovely note to say that he fully understood. He too had kids, and anyway it was not long since he himself had been one. We were welcome in the neighbourhood and he liked the way we were clearing our property and thereby improving the area. That one letter stood out. It eclipsed all the other anonymous possibilities that suggested that any one of our neighbours might have written us the letter. We were in. We were accepted. Unworthy though we were, we were part of the neighbourhood.

It wasn't until months later that we discovered that Jean was a brand-new Christian. Instinctively he was extending to us a welcome in Jesus' name.

To welcome is to take a loving initiative

To some of us love is a response, a reaction to a beautiful face, a kind nature, a good deed. We just can't help loving them. They call it forth from us, just as steak and chips call forth saliva. But Jesus' brand of love is not a response, but an initiative. It was while we were still sinners, enemies of God, that Jesus died as a supreme expression of God's love for us. His attitude to the people who abused him, whipped him, lied about him, crucified him, was not a reaction or a response. He stifled the attitude that was called forth from him and instead took the initiative and loved them. Mercifully his attitude to me is still the same.

To some of us a welcome is just a response. A stranger walks into your space and what can you do but smile and shake his hand?

Yet a welcome can also be an initiative. It is not that someone walks into your space and you are forced to react. They are just there. Their presence makes no call on you for a response. They are not friends; they are not enemies; they probably don't even know or care that you exist. They are just sitting out in the cold, not unwelcome, yet not welcome either. A welcome to someone like that is an unsolicited initiative that invades their isolation.

When I was twelve years old my parents sent me to boarding school. I loved home and the prospect of leaving it for a totally alien environment full of complete strangers filled me with unspeakable dread. My mother drove me down to the west of

England, where the school was located. With each passing mile my fear grew to the point that I was retching with apprehension. But my mum was wise and she knew that the best way of dealing with such fears was to get me out of reactive mode and into proactive.

'Justyn, I have a job for you, in fact it is a commission from the Lord Jesus. When you get to school and I have driven away and you are left alone, you will not really be alone. You will be surrounded by other new students who will be feeling exactly as you are feeling now. Jesus wants to make one of them feel OK, welcome, accepted. Your job is to find that person, to introduce yourself to him and make him feel welcome.'

Somehow the tide turned. I was no longer the victim of horrifying circumstances. I was the initiative-taker on a God-given mission. I could hardly wait to get there and for Mother to be on her way so I could get cracking on my search for this poor wretched boy who was feeling as bad as I had been previously.

But the parting was painful. For the first few minutes I felt desperately out of place. I didn't know where to go, who to talk to, what to do with my hands. Then I saw him, a boy with black hair and a spotty face, sitting awkwardly on a wall, his hands stuck deeply into his jacket pockets. Written all over his face were the same emotions that I was suffering. He hadn't seen me and his presence made no call upon me for a response. Except that the love and commission of Jesus inspired within me an initiative. I went up to him: 'Hello, are you new? . . . So am I. My name is Justyn. Let's be together.'

Bevis White was welcome, welcome in Jesus' name. And somehow, so was I.

At a wedding the other day I witnessed the same thing. Two members of our team were getting married and all was celebration, music, laughter and dancing. But there was one lady there a few years older than the youngsters who were peers of the bride and groom. She was divorced and that day's celebration must have been like salt in the wound. When the music started everyone jumped up to join a line dance. Well, not quite everyone. Kathy was still sitting at the table. No one had asked her to dance and she lacked the confidence to join the throng uninvited. She just sat there alone and I noticed a tear beginning to make its way down her cheek. What was I to do? I was a married man and my wife was my partner. And anyway, it was none of my business. Then I saw a handsome young man, very much the life and soul of the party, detach himself from the line and go up to her. I didn't hear what he said, but her face lit up and she joined the dance. Kathy was welcomed in Jesus' name.

Finding the grounds for the welcome mat

Andy and Stephanie had been living in their new cul-de-sac for three years before Alvin and Fiona moved in. They were second-generation neighbours. After only eighteen months the previous owners of that house had moved away. Money problems, probably. But having taken over the home of previously loved

neighbours, Alvin and Fiona were at a disadvantage.
Consequently they remained isolated. They didn't
play basketball. They didn't attend the pot-luck
suppers. Their kids didn't join in the Hallowe'en
celebration. They weren't the friendly type, but that's
OK because some people like to live their own lives.
Most neighbourhoods are entirely like that, where
neighbours just don't know each other, don't talk,
don't care, just mind their own business.

But Jesus was big in that neighbourhood, and
Jesus hates to see people he loves sitting out in the
cold. So Andy and Stephanie made it their business
to pray for some way of extending a welcome.

It was perhaps because they were lonely that Alvin
and Fiona delighted in the company of their golden
retriever. Rex welcomed them every time they came
home, not in Jesus' name but with great slobbery
licks. The neighbours might not have cared, but
Rex did.

But Alvin and Fiona faced a great dilemma when
the opportunity for two weeks in Hawaii came up.
What were they to do with Rex? He couldn't come
with them, but neither would they countenance the
thought of him staying in a cage at the local kennel
while they sunned themselves in Maui.

'Hi, Fiona,' called Stephanie one evening as Rex
relieved himself on the basketball stand while doing
walkies round the cul-de-sac. 'You look a little
down. Anything I can do to help?'

Of course it was Rex that was the cause of her
anguish. 'No problem,' said Stephanie. 'He can stay
with us. Our kids would love to have a dog around for
a couple of weeks.' And that's how it started. Alvin

and Fiona later welcomed Ferdinand the fish for a couple of weeks' stay while Andy and Stephanie were away. Now Alvin and Fiona had friends in the neighbourhood. They belonged. They were in. They were part of the neighbourhood. They were welcomed in Jesus' name.

Welcoming arms folded for fear of being swamped

I was invited recently to attend a church fellowship group to talk to them about evangelism. They met every other Thursday evening in a farmhouse on top of a hill. I arrived in a deluge of rain, feeling apprehensive and wishing I had stayed at home. I parked in the driveway and scuttled in out of the rain. But instantly the cloud lifted. There was a fire blazing. There was coffee. Someone had brought some muffins and date bread. The chairs were comfortable. It was not overcrowded. They were a nice friendly bunch of people who spent the first half-hour laughing hysterically. Immediately the world was not so bad. Then the meeting was called to order and I did my thing. Eventually I said something that turned out to be the most revolutionary thought of the whole evening, though it struck me as being almost too obvious to mention.

'Do you know what is the most compelling tool for evangelism you people have going for you?'

I let them guess, partly because that is good teaching technique, so I am told, and partly because I wanted to sneak another slice of date bread.

The best idea they came up with was their church, which has a brand-new sanctuary and a youthful pastor.

'No,' I disagreed. 'I think the best thing you have is what I have witnessed and felt this evening. Your friendship. Here I come as a complete stranger, and within three minutes I am glad to be here and jealous of what you enjoy week by week. If you could get some of your friends and neighbours who you are seeking to introduce to Jesus and sit them in the chair I have been occupying this evening, they would have powerful motivation to start seeking to know Jesus themselves.'

'Just what do you mean? Why is that so?'

'What you have is more than friendship. Yes, you obviously enjoy each other's company, but you are here for more than that. You have come with a serious agenda. If I were an unbelieving visitor I couldn't miss the fact that you are focusing on an invisible presence that you not only believe in, but evidently love. You talk to him as though you know him and you read the Bible as though it were true. What is more impressive still is that you act as though this invisible presence is interested in me. You ask me what I want him to do for me, then you talk to the invisible one as though he is sitting in the chair over there, asking him to address my specific needs. You talk in plain English. And, pardon my frankness, but you don't seem religious. You are real people.

'Now,' I concluded, 'how else could you convey all that to your friend without him even knowing it was going in?'

They ruminated on that for a while, while I ruminated on another slice of date loaf. Then they made a very telling confession. 'When we started to meet back in September, we agreed that twelve was the ideal size. Any more and we would be too full and too much of a crowd to be able to discuss properly and share openly. We therefore decided that we wouldn't invite others to join us.'

Oh, such tragedy! The very thing that was calculated to be the most friendly, loving expressing of the body of Jesus, the arms that could have reached out to encompass newcomers in welcome, were folded for fear of being swamped.

I couldn't bear it. 'What would happen if a new baby Christian, or even one not yet born, were to seek admittance to this group, but you said: "No. We have reached our optimum size"? On that basis you would be in danger of excluding Jesus himself from your gatherings. "I tell you the truth, unless you are converted and become like little children, you will never enter the kingdom of heaven. And whoever welcomes a little child like this in my name welcomes me."'

I had to reinforce the point, because cosy but closed fellowship groups which meet right in the place where the Church can most effectively welcome people are one of the greatest hindrances to taking on board newcomers. It is as though the entrances to the Church are choked with happy people having fellowship. So I continued mercilessly: 'Don't you remember how the earthly body of Jesus was pulled apart to receive sinners into God's family? His arms were nailed wide apart in welcome. Don't you see that the cost of introducing others to Jesus also required his body to go way beyond the limits of its comfort zone and to be crucified if necessary?'

They got the point and instantly set themselves to plan some guest events, starting with a Christmas evening in mid-December.

Where is the red carpet in your church?

To join something implies that you become part of it, you belong to it, you are known, recognised and welcomed into it. What is there that is joinable in the programme and structure of the average church? Sunday morning services are *attendable*, but hardly *joinable*. They are largely spectator sports. Anyway, it is difficult to join – to become part of, belong to, be known, recognised and welcomed into – a group of 150 people. But most churches do break down into smaller groupings. Sunday School classes, for example, are less daunting because class sizes are smaller. But the lecture hall atmosphere rarely fosters friendship, and once again is more attendable than joinable. Home fellowship groups are a much better environment to encourage others to join, for they meet in more congenial surroundings. They eat food and drink coffee. They are less lecture-oriented. But the trouble is that most groups are closed. They have met together for long enough to make any newcomer feel like an intruder, on the outside of an in-group. They have reached the optimum size for effective group dynamics and new additions threaten the chemistry. They have an agenda to seek the deeper things of God, to search out the mysteries of the Bible, and they want to be able to pray unhindered by an awareness that there are some present who don't know how to pray at all.

So where is the point of entry to the Church? Where does the red carpet lead to? Where is the church circle able to break hands long enough to fit in a newcomer?

I fear that we Christians have some repenting to do. While paying lip-service to the ideal of reaching out in love to the people around us, we remain in tight little cliques, sealed off by our theology, our traditions, our exclusivity. Ordinary people can't get past us, for instead of rolling out the red carpet of welcome we hang around the entrances to God's Kingdom, eagerly fellowshipping with each other while ignoring the people who want to get in. Jesus once said to Bible-loving people: 'Woe to you experts in the law, because you have taken away the key to knowledge. You yourselves have not entered, and you have hindered those who were entering.'

Welcoming a newborn, right where he lives

The group of neighbours which met in Brian and Dianne's home following the death of Brian's father didn't go unnoticed. 'Why is it that every Wednesday evening you people have some kind of gathering? Where do they all come from? What do you do?'

'We just meet to pray and read the Bible. We talk

about how we can be better parents and neighbours. That kind of stuff.' Then Brian would give an invitation to come along one Wednesday evening. 'It's open to anyone. No commitments. Just come and check it out for an evening.'

One Wednesday evening the phone rang just as Brian walked through the door after work. An unfamiliar voice introduced himself as Walter from up the street. Like other neighbours he was mystified by the regular gatherings. 'What goes on? What do you people do?' Brian explained. 'Well, can anyone come or is it a closed group?' Walter persisted.

'It certainly is not a closed group. People come from all over, but most are neighbours.'

'Well, could I come tonight?'

'Of course.'

'You see, I met God this week.' That got Brian's attention.

'What do you mean – you met God this week?'

'Can I come and explain? It's all so new to me that I don't know what to do with it. Could I just come and tell you what happened and then perhaps you could tell me where to start?'

'Fine, Walter. The group meets in a couple of hours' time, at 7.30.'

Three minutes later the door bell rang.

'Hi! I'm Walter. We were just talking on the phone, remember?'

Walter was so full of his new experience that he couldn't wait for the meeting, or even for the Dahls to eat their supper. He spilled out how he had been listening to a Christian programme on the radio and reading a Bible all on his own, when suddenly he

was not alone any more. He met Jesus right there
in his house. He told Brian and Dianne how he had
prayed: 'God, it's me, Walter! You know, from
Hilltop Avenue in Maple Ridge? I've just realised
that I'm not very nice to know, I think you'd call
me a sinner. But I do want you to be in my life.
Please help me.'

'That's fantastic!' said Brian, covering his emotions.
'Would you give a testimony tonight to the rest of the
group?'

Walter looked troubled. 'In all my fifty-six years
I have never heard that word. "Testimony" – what
does that mean? I'll gladly give one if I have one
to spare.'

The rest of the group were just as moved by
Walter's story. But it was his prayer that capped
it all. 'God, it's me again, Walter from up the street?
Sorry to keep bothering you, but I want to learn to
pray. I don't suppose I'll ever be able to pray like
these people, but I do want to get to know you.'

And that's how the body of Jesus grew in that
neighbourhood. One neighbour at a time being welcomed in Jesus' name into a family circle.

Kids on the welcome wagon

Children are wonderfully uninhibited. The concept of
taking the initiative to welcome others in Jesus' name
is no threat to them. Andy and Stephanie's four-year-
old daughter Tammy told her friend Andrea all about
Jesus. Andrea thinks she might like to know Jesus.
So Tammy tells her to ask him into her heart.

Paul, their six-year-old, brings Jamie home. Upstairs in his bedroom, Paul tells Jamie about Jesus and Jamie asks Jesus into his life.

Bob, their eight-year-old, prays for his whole class and has asked each one where they stand with Jesus.

Brian and Dianne's daughter Katherine was in grade seven when they moved into their new home. Adrienne, also in grade seven, lived over the street. She and Katherine became fast friends. Adrienne's home was not happy. She and her two older sisters were facing up to the likelihood that Mum and Dad were separating. Any friend of my daughter is a friend of mine, reasoned Brian, who went out of his way to befriend Adrienne's father, Murray, who was living in an apartment a few streets away. Against the rejection that she sensed at home, Adrienne felt welcome and acceptance from Katherine. Any friend of Katherine is a friend of mine, reasoned Adrienne as she received Jesus into her life. Mum and Dad and the two sisters attended Adrienne's baptism. A few weeks later the Dahls and Adrienne's whole family, even Murray, went on holiday together. They are all together now and moving towards the next step in full reconciliation – receiving Jesus as the head of the home.

Kids are inveterate welcomers. Perhaps that's why Jesus used a child as an object lesson for the vital task of welcoming in his name. 'Jesus took a little child and had him stand among them. Taking him in his arms, he said to them, "Whoever welcomes one of these little children in my name welcomes me; and whoever welcomes me does not welcome me but the one who sent me."'

Jesus loves Fred too much to leave him out in the cold

So what about Fred? Who will welcome him? The nearest church building is ten kilometres away and churches are not places where Fred would feel at home. But my home is right next door to his home. The people who regularly meet in my home represent the presence of Jesus, and were Fred to attend one of our meetings he would be blown away by the warmth of acceptance and welcome he would feel. So if he comes to my door, I will respond to his initiative by welcoming him. And even if he does not knock on my door, I will take the initiative to extend to Fred a welcome in Jesus' name. For Jesus' brand of welcome is not a response, but an initiative inspired by the truth that Jesus loves Fred too much to leave him sitting out in the cold.

9

Getting Down to Street Level

Praying in Jesus' name brings him closer to home

I will do whatever you ask in my name, so that the Son may bring glory to the Father. You may ask me for anything in my name, and I will do it . . . The Father will give you whatever you ask in my name.

Few people like to be preached at, but many people welcome an offer to be prayed for. The difference is probably in the agenda. The preacher has a sermon in mind while the pray-er has in mind the specific needs of the person he is praying for. So the person who approaches Fred with a sermon is likely to be rejected, while the one willing to pray for Fred's financial difficulties will be right on target.

Jesus was always on target. Of course he preached

sermons, but he approached people right where they were, in tune with their particular agenda. 'What do you want me to do for you?' he would ask. Suppose he asked that question of Fred. Fred might stall: 'Well, what sort of things do you have in mind? . . . make me nice? . . . make me like church? . . . help me to go to heaven when I die?' And Jesus would most likely reply: 'Whatever you ask in my name, I will do it!'

It's that 'whatever' that earths the whole thing, that removes Jesus from the religious mothballs we have wrapped him in and puts him right in the middle of the neighbourhood.

I find that when I have on my evangelist's hat I can readily talk to strangers about Jesus. But it is when my evangelist's hat is hung on its peg that it becomes more difficult. How do I introduce Jesus when out shovelling a manure pile with a neighbour? I'm not there on official evangelist business. And he's not there to be evangelised. We are just two men shovelling dung. That's when the 'whatever' comes in handy.

'Whatever' makes Jesus user-friendly

Charley was from San Francisco. He was a Vietnam veteran and had started a business fixing and installing furnaces and household heating systems. His marriage had ended and on the rebound he had married a Canadian wife. Johanna was younger and vivacious and the marriage was a great success. They moved to British Columbia, leaving a manager to run the business back in San Francisco. We attended sheep management classes together, and both decided that cattle would be much less aggravation. Their feet wouldn't need trimming; their wool wouldn't need cutting; they would require no dips in chemicals to kill the bugs; they could handle their own reproduction and births; coyotes and wolves wouldn't ravage them in the night. My uncle from Scotland told me that Highland cattle were idiot-proof, so we bought Highland. But even an idiot-proof reputation has certain limitations. Charley stretched the limits.

He came home from market one day with what he took to be a Highland bull. It was huge, with horns that stuck straight up in the air. Yes, it had a long shaggy coat, but there the similarity with Highlands ended. It was a mean beast which took delight in chasing Charley whenever he entered the field. Charley took revenge by chasing it round and round the field with his tractor. He finally decided to load it into his truck so he could take it to market before it killed him. He never did get it into the truck and he had to shoot it in the end.

Now I tell all that simply to establish Charley as a farmer who knew more about furnaces than he did about cattle. The barn with the broken back and the side I pulled in with my new bulldozer was a safety hazard and an eyesore. I had to get rid of it. A box of matches and a few gallons of diesel fuel were all that were needed, plus a few friends in case things got out of hand. Charley came, and Ron, together with a few other neighbours, for who can resist a good blaze? I picked a damp, drizzly day, but even so it was all over in half an hour; nothing left but ashes. Charley hadn't seen anything like it since Vietnam.

We were still standing there, leaning on pitchforks, admiring our handiwork, when Johanna drove up in their Jeep. 'Charley, there was a phone call a couple of hours ago from Bay Area Heating [one of their biggest customers in San Francisco] complaining that he cannot get hold of our office. So I called Marilyn, and it seems that Willie has done a bunk. The office is empty and some of the equipment is missing. He seems to have cut and run.'

'I'll have to go,' Charley apologised to me. 'I'll have to hop on a flight as quickly as possible so I can sort this mess out.'

'Just before you go, Charley, we should pray about it.'

'Hey, Justyn, you know me. I'm not a praying man.'

'Even so, Charley, Jesus is good at listening. Let's ask his help.'

'Well, OK.'

'So what do you want him to do about this situation?'

Charley had never shown any interest in religion to that point. Neither had any of the other neighbours who were there helping. It was rather special to see a little group of smoke-blackened fellows standing in a ring with their hats in their hands, praying together for God to help Charley sort out his business difficulties in San Francisco. The promise that Jesus would do whatever we asked in his name suddenly brought Jesus down to the level of barns and business in our neighbourhood.

Praying for neighbours by name brings surprising results

I previously made the point that few people who become Christians do so without someone somewhere having first prayed for them by name. Remember Arnold Fruchtenbaum?

When we moved into White Rock and were challenged to invite our neighbours to attend an evangelistic crusade, we realised to our chagrin that we didn't know our neighbours. They were all strangers to us. We took steps to remedy this situation by organising the 'Neighbourhood Watch' evening which provided us with a list of the names, addresses and phone numbers of all our neighbours. We started to use that list as a prayer list, praying regularly for our neighbours by name. We told no one that we were doing that. We just did it.

Al and Elisha Parker lived several houses away from us, down a long drive. They had two enormous dogs, a wise precaution against intruders. But their distance and their dogs meant that they were just names on our list. They never became friends. One day while walking past their house I noticed a furniture van at their door, so, risking a set of fangs in my backside, I ventured down the drive. 'We are moving to Kelowna,' they told me. 'We have rented a house, so we can see if we like Kelowna before burning our boats here in White Rock.'

So that was one set of neighbours we could scratch from our prayer list. If they were no longer our neighbours then we need no longer pray for them. What a waste of a whole year of praying for them by name! But then, we never expected anything to happen. We were only praying for them out of a sense of duty, of obedience to Jesus' teaching!

It was only six months later that we saw a furniture van back in their driveway. 'We didn't like Kelowna,' Al explained. 'But you people are Christians, aren't you? You'll be interested to know that while we were there we both became Christians.'

We expressed appropriate surprise. 'Do either of you come from Christian families? Do you have someone who was praying for you?'

'No. It was just out of the blue. This is all brand new for us and our family.'

When we moved to our present home and found such difficulty in fitting into the neighbourhood, it was Jean the helicopter pilot who unwittingly welcomed us. But what Jean and Julie didn't know was that we had been praying for them. We couldn't hold a neighbourhood watch session in this rural neighbourhood. It just didn't seem to fit. But in the natural course of events, we got to know about half the people who live up and down the street. Jean and Julie stuck out because they were in such bad odour with their neighbours, who didn't appreciate their stream running through the basement and missed the trees which once had held the bank together. So we prayed for them more fervently than for some of the others.

It was at a church Christmas meal some miles away that I discovered through conversation with someone at my table that they knew Jean and Julie. 'I really don't know them,' I confessed. 'I have

spoken to them on several occasions. In fact they
were very kind to us over a recent embarrassing
situation that arose in our neighbourhood. How do
you know them?'

'They just became Christians and they are in our
fellowship group.'

Life and death prayer

Brian and Dianne Dahl also developed a list of
neighbours. Their first approach was to plan the
neighbourhood barbecue, as I've already described.
But in preparation for the event they conducted a
survey so that each family would be able to make
their own special contribution to the meal. The list
they developed from the survey became their prayer
list. They asked whatever on behalf of whoever in
Jesus' name.

Antonio and Marie, being their next-door neighbours, were right at the top of the list. Their enthusi-
asm for the barbecue had shown no bounds. Marie
produced a huge bowl of home-made pasta. But
even when the event was all over, it was Antonio
and Marie who were determined to maintain the
friendship. They were for ever popping in or inviting
the Dahls over for a slice of pizza.

One day over cappuccino Antonio explained that
he and Marie were thinking of adopting a child.
In preparing the necessary paperwork they needed
someone to give them a character reference. Would
Brian and Dianne be willing to help?

Well, of course they were, and when all the forms

had been filled in and signed, Brian said: 'This is a very significant step you are taking. For us our children are special gifts from God. We had no choice when selecting them. God chose them for us and us for them. So why don't we take a moment now to pray that God will do the same for you, that he will choose the right child for you and make you right for the child?'

Antonio and Marie were very touched by the love and care shown by Brian and Dianne, but they were stirred deeply by the realisation that Jesus might get involved in their lives at this very special point.

The Dahls also prayed for Ian and Lee, who lived opposite. Ian was a sports fanatic whose satellite dish sucked in sports reports from all over the universe. One night, while fine-tuning his receiver, Ian sat back on the edge of his coffee table, not the best resting-place considering that it had a glass top. The glass shattered and Ian fell through. A shard of glass cut him deeply from wrist to elbow. Lee ran to the phone and called emergency, and within minutes the ambulance was on the scene. But Ian was bleeding profusely and before they could move him the paramedics gave him three units of blood.

Brian and Dianne, alerted by the flashing lights and the commotion, went over to see if they could help. Lee was distraught. It was touch and go whether they would be able to save Ian's life.

'Lee, Dianne and I will pray. We are confident that the Lord Jesus will help.'

Ian didn't die. He came home three days later with his arm all strapped up.

'How are you feeling, Ian?' Brian enquired when he went over for a visit.

'Glad to be alive. Hey, I hear you were praying for me. That's very special. Thanks. I suppose the big man in the sky must have heard you.'

Praying where the rubber meets the road

One of the definite advantages to establishing a group of neighbours who regularly meet in Jesus' name is that it facilitates agreed prayer in the neighbourhood. In addition to promising that he would give us whatever we might ask in his name, Jesus further assured us: 'If two of you on earth agree about anything you ask for, it will be done for you.'

When we established a neighbourhood group in White Rock, we made it our practice to pray about specific needs we were aware of in the area. Every few months we would walk round the neighbourhood, visiting each home. We reminded them that there was in operation a neighbourhood prayer group at which they were very welcome. However, we understood that people live busy lives and that even if they were not able to come we would love to hear from them by phone should any special need arise for which they would like prayer. Everyone was politely appreciative of the visit and the offer, though few attended the group. But the seed was planted.

Down the street lived a Japanese family. They never attended the group, but he loved to play golf, so from time to time we played a round.

Then their teenage daughter was diagnosed with
leukaemia. They phoned and the group got down
to agreed prayer on their behalf in Jesus' name. For
months we wrestled with God for that young lady.
It would make a much better story had she been
miraculously healed, but this is real life. To our great
grief she died. But it was members of our group and
the church they attended who were there to help the
family with their grief.

Roger, a neighbour of Brian and Dianne, broke
his leg in a motor cycle accident. For some reason
it just would not heal. After sixteen months of being
off work, it appeared that he would never mend. The
job at Safeway that had been kept for him was about
to be passed on to a replacement. 'Would you get
the group to pray that God will fix my leg?'

Agreed prayer was made in Jesus' name. Next
week Roger had yet another x-ray. 'Your leg is
mending,' pronounced the doctor. 'You can go back
to work as soon as you feel up to it.'

Jesus had come down to street level.

Andy and Stephanie's group was less planned, but
just as real. They didn't make it known that there was
a neighbours' group praying each week for the good
of the neighbourhood, the reason being that they
didn't need to make it known. Everyone already
knew. 'Neighbours that play together, probably will
also pray together', to do further violence to the
ancient proverb.

When a child up the street was due to go into
hospital for a heart operation, the family phoned
to ask for prayer. That set a precedent such that
when another child was suffering from a tumour in

a shoulder, Andy and Stephanie were again asked to pray. Jesus was big in that neighbourhood, and who in their right minds would not ask help from someone who freely offered to do whatever they might ask in his name? It wasn't a church doing religious things behind stained glass windows, praying for the suffering, the down-trodden and the poor. It was neighbours, asking specific 'whatevers' on behalf of other neighbours, in Jesus' name.

And the ripples are still spreading out. Several of the neighbourhood children, including Andy and Stephanie's three, attend the local primary school. So why shouldn't Jesus be big there also?

Stephanie called together several neighbourhood mums and joined a 'Mums Who Care' group. They meet regularly on school property to pray for the staff and children of Mountain Park Primary. The principal was initially a little cool towards the plan, but forbidding it would have been churlish. So it was tolerated. Just before Christmas the Mums Who Care group laid on a special lunch for the frazzled teachers. It wasn't an extra event, just something they did in the staff room during the lunch hour. It was beautifully done and well received by the whole staff. No one made a speech, or prayed a prayer or gave out a tract. But on every table there was a card saying: 'This lunch is laid on by "Mums Who Care", a group of women who meet weekly to pray for the school. Their prayer is that this Christmas Jesus will fill you all with his wisdom, strength and joy.'

The principal is no longer cool in her acceptance of the group. She is warm and friendly and knows where to turn when there are things for which she needs help from above, 'whatevers' that can be passed on in agreement in Jesus' name.

It is the 'whatever' promise that invites Jesus to come and live at street level in my neighbourhood, right where the rubber hits the road.

10

Keeping the Focus

Worshipping in Jesus' name makes him the focus of attention

God inhabits the praises of his people . . . Therefore speak to one another with psalms, hymns and spiritual songs . . . giving thanks . . . in the name of our Lord Jesus Christ.

We love because he first loved us. If anyone says, 'I love God,' yet hates his brother, he is a liar . . . Everyone who loves the father loves his child as well. This is how we know that we love the children of God: by loving God and carrying out his commands. This is love for God: to obey his commands.

Do you love me? . . . Feed my sheep.

The ferry takes just over an hour and a half to cross the Georgia Strait which separates Vancouver Island from the mainland. It passes through a scattering of islands. The sea is alive with wildlife and the seagulls and bald eagles swoop to snatch up its bounty. Tourist cameras click and whirr, while locals snore. I never get tired of the trip, but occasionally sleep does get the better of me. On one such occasion I was awakened from slumber by an announcement over the public address system. I was too far gone to hear what was said, but the reaction of my fellow passengers could not be ignored. To a man they all went to the port side of the ferry, causing the vessel to list in an alarming manner. Curiosity got the better of me and I struggled to my feet and joined the back of the throng. I may not have heard what was said over the PA, but the focused attention of several hundred people was irresistible. They were all looking at something and pointing excitedly. I couldn't see anything, so I climbed on to a life raft to see over their heads. There was a pod of killer whales keeping pace with the ferry, rising and dipping, their black and white bodies effortlessly gliding through the water.

If I want to introduce Fred to Jesus, it may well help him if I invite him along to a worship service where the invisible Jesus is the focus of the attention of several hundred people.

Experts on church growth tell us that the Sunday morning service is one of the best evangelistic opportunities of the whole week. It seems that people who have any kind of church background understand that people do religious stuff at 10.30 on a Sunday morning! Therefore, any individual with the slightest inclination towards doing religious stuff will do so at the prescribed hour and in the place labelled 'church'.

So down they sit in the pew and watch all the

strangeness unfolding around them! Mercifully for them, they are not the centre of attention. In a specifically evangelistic service the focus is on the poor unsuspecting unbeliever who has been suckered into attending by his Christian friend. But in a Sunday morning service the focus is on God, on worshipping him. So the visiting unbeliever is able to relax (to some extent) and witness a few hundred people focusing their attention on an invisible presence.

The man at the front speaks on behalf of the whole assembly to the invisible one. The choir stands up and with great polish (indicating how much they care) they sing love songs to thin air. Then the whole assembly sings songs of devotion to the one that none of them can see, yet the love that many individuals feel is clearly expressed, not just by the words that the songs put on their lips but by their body language. They lift their hands and a look of joy comes over their faces. What is it that turns on so many relatively sane people? Then the Bible is read and people seem to believe it, for the man at the front bases a thirty-minute lecture on it and the people take notes as though what he was saying really mattered!

Most important of all is the sense of the presence of God. Where the body of Jesus comes together, the presence of Jesus is evident. Where they focus their loving worship on him, the presence of Jesus is unmistakable. He inhabits the praises of his people.

Worship can send mixed messages

I used to host a weekly radio programme via Trans

World Radio that was beamed from Monte Carlo all over Europe. It was fun putting it together, for I recorded it all on the streets of London. Armed with my little tape recorder I would interview the people I encountered. I talked with politicians, TV personalities, sports heroes, but most of the time I talked with the ordinary man on the street – for that is who one tends to meet while on the street (though as often as not it was the ordinary woman in the street, but somehow that conjures up the wrong impression!).

One week I wandered into St Paul's Cathedral. It was a great place for interviews, for the tourists were all in pensive mood, wandering round marvelling at the wonders of Sir Christopher Wren's design. But it was more than that. There was a sense of the awesome presence of God, for that great cathedral is a place where God regularly inhabits the praises of his people.

I spotted one likely subject for an interview, who turned out to be an American student doing some courses at the London School of Economics. 'What does this cathedral make you think about God?' I asked her.

'God must be very great, an awe-inspiring being, to have called forth such beauty from those who worship him.'

Of course not everybody receives the same message. I sidled up to one young man from Yorkshire. 'What does this cathedral make me think about God?' he repeated. 'It's a bloody museum! God must have been dead for a very long time by the looks of it.'

Oh well! You can't win them all.

But it is not just architectural worship that can be misinterpreted. The current trends in worship in North America are rather strange. Worship events are often as unpredictable as the wind. Great! Predictable worship is uncreative, boring and dry. The wind of God's Spirit blows wherever he wants to, and for man to seek to control him is as inappropriate as it is impossible.

Strange happenings in worship events are nothing new, for even in the New Testament it is clear that there were strange goings on. In the same context as the famous passage about love, Paul describes a worship event which is moved by the Spirit of God to the point of unpredictable weirdness. But, ever mindful of the unbeliever, Paul fears for the reaction of someone wandering in off the street. 'Will he not say that you are out of your mind?' So he makes a pitch for worship to be user-friendly for the unbeliever, such that 'he will fall down and worship God, exclaiming, "God is really among you!"'

I recall a university mission I was involved in some years back. In preparation for the mission some members of the Christian Union felt that the powers of darkness should be driven back from the Student Union building. They were inspired by the precedent of King Jehoshaphat, whose army was preceded by a worshipping choir. All that would be required of the soldiers would be to 'stand firm and see the deliverance the Lord would give them'. So the Christian students moved into the central atrium of the Student Union building at peak hour and started to worship God. That would have been wonderful but for their style of worship, which was extreme. I greatly admired their zeal, but was saddened by the reaction of their fellow students. Like Paul's imaginary intruder, they thought these Christians were out of their minds and, far from falling down to worship God, they wanted nothing to do with them or the up-coming mission.

Quite clearly there is a balance here. David's worship of God when the Ark of the Covenant was being carried to Jerusalem was over the top, according to his wife. So caught up was he in the wonder of God that David danced before him regardless of who might be watching – 'user-friendly' be blowed! There is a time to be so lost in 'wonder, love and praise' that only God matters. But this book is about introducing Jesus to our neighbourhood, and in this context I am with Paul in sensitivity to what Fred may think of my style of worship. Don't misunderstand me, I am not ashamed to worship God in any style, neither do I feel that worship should only happen behind the closed doors of the church. I firmly believe that the joyful worship of God is contagious and I want Fred to get caught up in it and drawn in. Yet I most definitely do not want Fred to be repulsed by my style, the manner of my worship.

A church structured towards worshipping God in the neighbourhood

When Andy and Stephanie moved to Mountain Park, their first intention had been to continue as members of Kingsway Chapel. But it soon became apparent that this would be impractical. They found Longview Community Church, where the pastor welcomed them enthusiastically. He promised to pray for them as they made their own neighbourhood the focus of their attention.

More than that, the pastor used Andy and Stephanie's initiative to inspire others to do likewise. He built the whole emphasis of the church around small neighbourhood groups, insisting that the groups were not there to support the church. Rather, the church was there to support the groups.

That is a radical rethink. The local church is more the local church when it meets as a small group in a neighbourhood than it is when it meets as a congregation on a Sunday morning. Longview Community Church now requires that anyone offering themselves to become a church council member must be a leader, or at least an active member, of a neighbourhood group.

All neighbourhood group leaders meet once a month for a time called 'Focus'. And focus it does, on God in worship, then on neighbours in love. The meeting starts with a time of worship, expressing to God how much they all love him. Then they move on to a time of reporting on what has been happening in each neighbourhood group. This gives a sense of accountability, the realisation that others care what you are about in your own small corner. But, more important, it gives huge encouragement. 'Hey, you'll never guess what happened last week in our street!' and before you know it they are all swapping anecdotes, so that between them they could write a book like this every month! They leave as pumped up as a crowd of football hooligans after the home team has won. But not before someone has injected some practical 'how to' teaching on some aspect of being good neighbours.

So home they all go, back to their neighbourhoods with their faces aglow from having gazed on God in worship and realised afresh that to worship God is to love your neighbour.

'Glory to God in the highest' (and on the street)

Andy and Stephanie first invited me to their neighbourhood in this context. They wanted to do something that would focus the attention of their neighbours on Jesus, who was big in that cul-de-sac! Christmas was coming, when even agnostics pay some attention to the baby in the manger, so they decided that the season would give them just the opportunity they needed. I was free to come on the December Friday evening they wanted, so they printed invitations and started baking. Jonathan and Melody were professional bakers: the food would be no major hassle.

Then they made their first mistake. Stephanie and Melody set out to go round the neighbourhood to knock on every door and hand-deliver the invitation. Something about doing that, coupled with a nervousness at promoting the first specifically Christian event in their neighbourhood, made them feel unnatural. But their neighbours were good enough friends to tell them honestly what was wrong. Lois the ex-nun voiced it. 'You two look guilty, coming to my door like a couple of Jehovah's Witnesses. What's the matter with you?'

But however they delivered the invitations, everyone in the entire neighbourhood came. When I arrived I came with a sense of walking on holy ground. I had heard about what they were doing in that neighbourhood. And as I parked my car under a street lamp in the cul-de-sac, there were the famous basketball hoops, looking a little rusty. The house was jammed with friendly people, all good friends and thoroughly enjoying being together. Stephanie warned me that some were rather suspicious. She pointed Lois out to me. She was sitting with her arms tightly folded, body language shouting rejection at me.

When everyone was well fed and watered, Andy made the introduction. He explained that as it was Christmas, some of them had felt that to do something which specifically reflected the reason for the season would be an appropriate thing. 'So we have asked Justyn Rees, a story teller, to tell us the traditional story of Christmas.'

To begin with they were more nervous than I was. But gradually they thawed, then laughed and cried with me as we relived the events of the first Christmas through the eyes of some of the principal characters. Even Lois unfolded her arms near the end. For nearly an hour the whole neighbourhood focused on the baby in the manger, and the shepherds weren't the only ones with tears trickling down their grubby old cheeks beside the manger. The tiny baby was big in that neighbourhood as he inhabited the praises of a group of neighbours.

When it was over and we were all having seconds of mulled wine, Sam and Pauline introduced themselves as living at the far end of the cul-de-sac, 'just opposite where you turn the corner to leave'. They told me that they were deeply moved by the story, which they had never heard told as though it were true. It was always presented in the context of children in dressing-gowns pretending to be shepherds, with angels swinging on wires suspended from the ceiling. 'Would you be willing to come to our house next week and tell the same story for all our friends? We have family members and people at work who, like us, have never heard this kind of stuff.'

So a week later another house full of agnostics worshipped at the manger, and the presence of Jesus, inhabiting the praises of that houseful, was big in the neighbourhood.

Gifts complement each other

Russ and Sandy Rosen are called to be worship leaders. They love God and use their musical gift to draw others into the celebration of who he is. We teamed up a few years back. I was unsure at first just how well the gifts of evangelist and worship leader would mix. We debated the validity of putting words of worship into the mouths of people who didn't even believe in God. I advocated the seeker-sensitive approach, while they argued that as love for God is the thing to which we are calling people, then worship of God should be front and centre in all we do.

We formed a team of musicians who travelled with us on a five-year pilgrimage across Canada, and around us we built our Band Wagon, the mobile theatre that we set up on car parks and street corners from Vancouver to Newfoundland. And there we worship God in a style that resembles a street party. It is the exuberant joy of the Lord Jesus that draws people in, gets them up on their feet dancing and warms their hearts to love God. My job is to speak, and it is the preaching of Jesus that inspires faith. Their job is to sing, and it is the worship of God that inspires love. So the job of the evangelist and the job of the worshipper do in fact complement each other perfectly, the one inspiring faith, the other inspiring love.

On several occasions Russ and Sandy have joined us in neighbourhood events. Most recently we did an Easter happening. I told the story of Easter while they sang it. My words and their songs were both a proclamation of Jesus, inspiring faith. And the worship in the words of the characters through whom I told the story was evident. 'My Lord and my God!' worshipped Thomas. 'Precious Lord' worshipped Russ and Sandy. The occasion was wholeheartedly directed towards God in worship, yet no one said, 'You are out of your mind.' And the love for God that inspired the good food and the whole friendly occasion was pleasing to our heavenly Father and caused some to say, 'God is really among you!'

Words are cheap. Actions cost

The heart of what Jesus wanted from Peter was love. 'Do you love me?' he asked three times, and each time Peter said 'Yes', Jesus responded, 'Then feed my sheep.' The inference is that if you love God, then the way you express it is in loving action towards those he loves.

'Love the Lord your God with all your heart, soul, mind and strength' is clearly the greatest commandment and the highest ideal for any human being to focus on. Yet in all the Bible there are only one or two references to anybody saying the words to God, 'I love you.' Peter said it three times and the psalmist said it once. Why are there not more examples of people saying those special words of supreme worship? It must have something to do with the manner in which God wants us to express our love for him, in action more than in words. 'This is love for God: to obey his commands.' Yet the danger is that sometimes we can get so engrossed in the actions that loving God once inspired that we lose the heart of it all – loving God. The Ephesian church was full of loving actions, good deeds, hard work, perseverance, endurance. Yet God held it against them that they had lost their first love. He therefore called them to repent: not of their good deeds, for he told them to 'do the things they did at first'. It was their loveless hearts for which they were to repent.

I am terrified lest I get so wrapped up in doing good stuff in my neighbourhood that my love for God gets choked. Fred will never be drawn into the worship of God while I bombard him with good deeds from a cold heart.

So Jesus puts the question to me, as he put it to Peter: 'Do you love me? . . . Then feed my sheep.' 'Do you love me? . . . Then do something loving for Fred.'

11

Making the Connection

Uniting in Jesus' name makes him credible

If you are offering your gift at the altar and there remember that your brother has something against you, leave your gift . . . First go and be reconciled to your brother.

By this all men will know that you are my disciples, if you love one another.

May they be brought to complete unity to let the world know that you sent me and have loved them even as you have loved me.

From Jesus the whole body, joined and held together, grows and builds itself up in love.

It is true to say that the arms and legs, head and trunk that connect to form my body are actually the members of Jesus' body. It is also true to say that my individual body is but one member of half a dozen other bodies that together are connected in my neighbourhood to be the body of Jesus; which in turn is but one member of the body of Jesus in Mount Lehman; which is but a small part of the worldwide Church which is the body of Jesus.

Connectedness is very important. To hold someone's hand can be very warm and reassuring, provided of course that the hand is still connected to the arm and the arm to the body!

The Bible offers no place for a dismembered finger to point in accusation at the rest of the body for its failures and shortcomings. Fingers can only scratch the exact right spot when connected to the part that itches!

I fear that such mental images of dismembered parts of the body are a bit nauseating, but is it any the less disgusting to see individuals breaking away from their local church with the mistaken idea that they can be more effective by going it alone? Is it any less a dismemberment of the body of Jesus to see whole congregations disassociating themselves from their denomination in order to remain pure? Yes, a severed hand in a bottle of formaldehyde can be very pure, but it doesn't help to hold it when you are feeling off colour.

The Bible uses a similar analogy, but in rather better taste than mine! Jesus spoke of a vine which exists to bear fruit. He is the actual vine, we are the branches, and the fruit we bear brings glory to the vine and the vine dresser. But he stresses that any break between the main stem of the vine and the extremities of the twigs where the fruit is borne will cause fruitlessness through disconnection from the life source. Any break in the branches or limbs or twigs is fatal to the fruit.

Certainly the Church has its shortcomings. As a body it suffers from 'spots, wrinkles and blemishes', to quote the apostle Paul who, I suppose, also sometimes used nauseating images to convey his message. But pimples, warts and all, God hasn't finished with us yet! For all our imperfections as a body, those who seek amputation as a means of putting distance between themselves and the blemishes of the rest of the body will end up far more spotty and wrinkled through decomposition than they ever were while still connected!

All this is important because in order to make Jesus credible in my neighbourhood, I must be connected to the whole body of Jesus worldwide. Fred will never take Jesus seriously if he limps up our street as an amputee.

God's love through Jesus is made believable by our unity

The credibility of Jesus is seriously undermined in many communities by the divisions that persist between the churches. Jesus taught that his mission as one sent by God to love the world would be made credible by the unity of his body. 'May they be brought to complete unity to let the world know that you sent me and have loved them even as you have loved me.'

In 1995 a small group of us set off on a cross-Canada pilgrimage for reconciliation. We set ourselves the goal of travelling from coast to coast in five years, and in that time to visit as many communities as possible. We purchased a set of rusty articulated trailers and converted them to form a mobile theatre seating some three hundred people. There every night we would sing, dance, act and story-tell the gospel. Our theme was clearly reconciliation: reconciliation between man and God and reconciliation between man and man. It has been a fascinating exercise to visit town after town. Each is different. Some towns are wide open and people readily respond to the good news that God loves them. But in other places the people are closed.

One town sticks out in my memory, a fishing community on the west coast. We were invited there by the ministerial association, a community of a dozen churches of several denominations. They found us a plum site, right in the middle of town in the car park of the main shopping centre. No one could fail to notice our brightly coloured Band Wagon, for it was right by the bus terminal and the ferry terminal and on the main street. But nothing happened. We were there for a whole month. Numbers of people came, but zero response.

In meeting with several of the pastors it became apparent that something was amiss. The pastor of the biggest church in town was not on speaking terms with the other pastors. I phoned him so that we might introduce ourselves to him, but he would not meet me. 'We weren't in favour of your coming and so there is nothing for us to discuss.'

'But half our team are from your denomination,' I pleaded. 'They are young people and they just don't understand why we need be disconnected.'

Then it came out that the issues were theological. Over the phone he told me how hurt he had been by the attitude of some of the other pastors who had, as he put it, 'jumped on the signs and wonders band wagon. They think I am unspiritual just because people don't fall down slain in the Spirit during my services. We have been receiving refugees from several of the other town churches, people who are driven away by strange goings on.'

'And you think that we are tarred with the same brush?'

'I don't know what you are, but we have to be careful.'

So I phoned the pastor of the state-of-the-art charismatic church in town and invited him out for breakfast at McDonald's. I got the same story in reverse. 'He's so stuck in his traditional ways that none of us can get through to him. Our responsibility is to move along with the Spirit, not to judge others in their walk.'

Yet another pastor confided in me that there had been an initial coming together of several churches as they sought to ride the crest of the wave of this new move of God. But the last few months had brought nothing but arguments and the fellowship between the churches was at an all-time low.

Little wonder that few people from that town would take seriously Jesus' claim to be an expression of the Father's love to them. No amount of programmes or buildings or literature or Band Wagon events or signs and wonders would ever take the place of the oneness of Jesus' body as the hallmark of the truth of the gospel. Jesus' credibility was blown in that town, for he could offer the people nothing but amputated body parts.

So we ceased to preach the gospel in the Band Wagon and concentrated on an expression of repentance for our dividedness as a church, and a beautiful thing happened.

The day after we were scheduled to leave that town there was to be a referendum in the province of Quebec to decide whether they wanted to separate from the rest of Canada to become an independent nation. Everyone was feeling as though we were facing national divorce. The ministerial association resolved to call a meeting of all the Christians in town to pray for the unity of the country. They rented the local theatre, neutral turf and a good central location.

It was Sunday evening, the night before the referendum. A couple of hundred people turned up, but there was an awkwardness, for they were not in fellowship. It was then that the miracle happened. One pastor stood up on the stage and said; 'How can we pray for our country to be unified if our town is not at one? And how can we expect our town to be unified while the churches are not at one? I want all of you to know that before God I repent of my sin in permitting this state of affairs to continue to this day. I repent of my party spirit, my exclusive denominationalism, my theological pride, my superior attitude towards our style of worship. May God have mercy on me.' Then another pastor followed suit. Pretty soon there were ten pastors lined up on the stage, one after another voicing repentance for lack of unity and disconnectedness. The churches weren't all there. The biggest church in town ran their own show that evening in competition to what the other churches were doing. Nevertheless, something changed that night.

We decided to hold over the Band Wagon for two extra nights to cover referendum night on Monday and Hallowe'en on Tuesday. We preached the gospel of how dearly God loved the people of that town and we told them that the coming of Jesus was the supreme expression of that love. And people believed us! For the first time since we had arrived they believed us and they responded to the message. The oneness of his body made credible Jesus' mission as God's emissary of love.

Disconnected Christians are like loose cannons

Exactly the same principle applies to individual members of Jesus' body or small groups of members who are not connected. These are loose cannons careening around the lower decks as the Church is tossed this way and that by the fashionable waves of fresh doctrinal emphasis. They destroy church after church, causing havoc in the name of spirituality, knowing no restraint or accountability. These people bring the name of Jesus into disrepute and render him incredible wherever they go.

Part of a big, loving, creative entity – the body of Jesus

When Andy and Stephanie moved to Mountain Park, they acted wisely. Finding that their connectedness with their city church was strained by distance and the conflicting agendas of neighbourhood and church, they realised that changes would have to be made. With the blessing of their former church, they sought out a local church in Langley and quickly identified with it. Consequently everything they do as a small neighbourhood group is in fellowship with what the rest of the body of Jesus is doing. They are not isolated or amputated from all the other wonderful things that the Church is doing all around them. They are part of a big, loving, creative entity – the body of Jesus.

A 'Focus on the Family' parenting self-help group was established in a hall near their home. Stephanie recruited for it at her next basketball game. Several struggling parents eagerly joined.

Youth for Christ started a Tae Kwon Do group for teenagers. Andy was quick to make it known to some of the teens in the neighbourhood, who learned martial arts and spiritual arts concurrently! The Baptist church nearby held a youth event weekly called 'Wildlife'. Several of the less pugnacious teens joined that.

Another nearby church opened a pre-school playgroup. Stephanie linked several toddlers and mums with that group. And this proved an excellent connection with the holiday Bible club that another group came to help run right in the neighbourhood – 'Wonderfare'.

Keats Camp, a summer island paradise for teens, became the summer activity for neighbourhood secondary school kids, particularly for Andy and Stephanie's baby-sitter Mike, for that's where he became a Christian.

And Mike's father became a Christian a year later when Andy and Stephanie's church, in partnership with Campus Crusade for Christ, distributed to each home in the neighbourhood copies of a video showing the life of Jesus. So the following Sunday Mike, his father and mother set off together for the United Church.

Owned by the neighbourhood, connected to the Church

Andy and Stephanie are responsible members of a local congregation. Jonathan and Melody are members of another. The group, however, belongs to the neighbourhood and while it is encouraged and fostered by several churches, it is not owned or controlled by any one church, for it operates interdenominationally.

Some church leaders are threatened by this, fearing that it will detract from their own particular church agenda and that down the road there may well be anarchy as everyone does what is right in his own eyes. 'Where is the accountability?' they argue.

Yet Andy and Stephanie are accountable, for they are members of a local church. And the group is connected, for they operate as part of the tapestry of the beautiful picture that all the local churches are weaving together to the glory of God.

'What about sheep stealing?' quavers the critic.

The experience of that particular group is that sheep are not stolen, but rather are returned to the fold of their origin. Several of the neighbours who have become active Christians through that neighbourhood group had previous Christian roots. There were lapsed Catholics, Anglicans, and United Church members, all of whom were inspired to seek out their original denomination and rejoin it. True, there were some who were drawn into Longview Community Church where Andy and Stephanie were members, but these had no previous church connections. And true, a whole row in that church is taken up by a group of exceptionally good friends – Andy and Steph's neighbours, who once went nowhere.

The arms of love with which Jesus hugs Andy and Stephanie's neighbours are firmly connected to the rest of his body and consequently his loving overtures are credible.

12

Telling the Truth

Talking in Jesus' name generates faith

How can they call on the one they have not believed in? And how can they believe in the one of whom they have not heard? . . . Consequently, faith comes from hearing the message, and the message is heard through the word of Christ.

'Sticks and stones can break my bones, but words can never hurt me!' That's one way of looking at it. 'The pen is mightier than the sword!' That's quite another. Those proverbs are full of contradictions. I can't think why anyone takes them seriously!

The Bible is full of words – God's words.

Words are fundamental to creation, for even the visible creation became reality through words. By faith we understand that the universe was formed at God's command, so that what is seen was not made out of what was visible, but by God's word alone. The visible was made from the audible. Reality sprang from words. People who understand this have a special handle on life, for 'blessed are those who have not seen and yet have believed'.

In fact, all through the ages it has been those who understood and were prepared to operate on the conviction of what they heard, rather than what they saw, who were rewarded. The Bible gives dozens of examples of godly people who lived their whole lives uniquely by faith in the evidence of their ears, without ever actually seeing the reality of the thing they were believing for, the fulfilment of the promises. They only heard about them and welcomed them from a distance. They were all commended for their faith, yet none of them actually received what had been promised.

What was it that enabled these people to base their whole lives, not on the evidence of their eyes, but rather on the evidence of their ears? Answer: they were sure of what they hoped for and certain of what they did not see. In short, they had faith.

So if Fred is to relate to God by faith, how can you help him find it?

God's promises give substance for hope; visualisation spreads a mist of wishful thinking

Faith is a gift and God is the only giver of that gift. If you try to give the gift of faith from your own resources you will come up with a second-rate human substitute – wishful thinking.

New Age philosophy is everywhere. In the classroom children are being taught to close their eyes and visualise whatever they want. Educators believe that what you see with your mind's eye is the creative force to make that vision a reality. Sick people are taught to visualise healing to the affected parts of their anatomy. Salespeople stick salary-level goals to their car steering wheels. Pictures of yachts are stuck to refrigerator doors. All these objectives are the things hoped for. By faith people reach out towards these things because they hope for them, long for them, dream of owning that yacht, earning that money, being that kind of person. And does it work? Yes, I suppose it must do.

Even the Church has adopted the same kind of techniques. Visualise, verbalise, actualise. You'll hear Christian preachers expounding that gospel. 'Picture in your mind's eye the answer to your prayers, never doubting that there will be a fulfilment, and you won't be disappointed.' Perhaps God could take a few months' holiday and nobody would notice! The system might still work just as well in his absence.

But is that the Christian gospel? No, but it has some striking similarities. It may help to lay New Age thinking and Christian faith alongside each other.

The New Ager sees a vision in his mind's eye. The Christian sees a vision in his mind's eye.

The New Ager likes what he sees and hopes for it. The Christian likes what he sees and hopes for it.

The New Ager moves towards the reality of his hope with expectancy. The Christian moves towards the reality of his hope with expectancy.

But there the similarity ends.

The New Ager has nothing but his own imagination with which to paint the original vision. However, the Christian has God's word, which paints a vision far more wonderful than anything we could ever ask or think.

The New Ager has nothing but his own creativity to turn the vision into reality. The Christian has the omnipotent Spirit of God, who gives life to what is written.

The New Ager's vision is like plastic with which his imagination seeks to mould a reality. The Christian's heart is like warm, moist soil in which the seed of God's word germinates by the Spirit and grows into the reality that God intends.

The Christian's vision is not the product of his own imagination, his own wishful thinking. It is the promise of God that paints the vision in the believer's mind. It's not his prayer that bends God's will to conform to his vision, rather it is God's will that bends his praying to line up on God's promise. So as the Christian's will becomes attuned to God's will, the Christian begins to get excited about what he hears. He develops a longing for that which God is promising and it becomes his hope. Then faith takes over and he makes a definite choice to believe the promises he hopes for. That is when the Spirit of God goes to work and the words which spelled out the promises spring into reality, just as did creation when God said: 'Let there be . . .'

If we are going to give Fred something to get excited about, a hope he can believe in, a vision that will lead to reality, we have to tell him the truth of Jesus. Otherwise he will paint his own pictures of Jesus in his own mind and the object of his worship will be an idol of his own creation. Our job is to communicate the promises of God as clearly, as accurately and as attractively as possible. God's part is to give to Fred a hope that will make him long for those promises to come true for him personally, the faith to expect them and finally the Spirit's power to make it all happen.

Verbalisation, not visualisation

I have stressed this point for fear that someone will accuse me of attempting to introduce people to Jesus through the power of visualisation. Verbalisation is key to helping Fred, not visualisation. Faith comes by hearing, not by seeing.

The day after the feeding of the five thousand, a crowd of spongers tracked Jesus down, hoping for another free meal. When he told them to have faith in him they asked him, 'What miraculous sign then will you give that we may see it and believe you? What will you do? Our forefathers ate the manna in the desert; as it is written: "He gave them bread from heaven to eat."'

Jesus' response shocked them: 'I am the bread of life. He who comes to me will never go hungry, and he who believes in me will never be thirsty. But as

I told you, you have seen me and still you do not believe.'

Here was a crowd of people before whose very eyes Jesus had performed unmistakable miracles. He had pulled five thousand fish sandwiches out of one kid's lunchbox. This was not mere wishful thinking; they had the evidence of their eyes and their stomachs to prove it. Yet still they did not believe.

I must confess that I don't much trust the evidence of my own eyes. When I watch a movie on TV I am well aware of the visual tricks that clever producers can play. I don't believe what I see, and no one expects me to do so. Then on comes the news and, sitting in my own living-room, sipping my goodnight hot chocolate, I see footage of starving people and mutilated bodies from the latest battle front. But I don't vomit or weep. I have learned to treat the evidence of my eyes as unreality. Next comes the TV preacher. He calls up needy people and prays for them and a cripple throws his crutch across the stage and a blind person reads from the Bible. But I don't believe what I see for I know that clever producers can play tricks with my eyes. Then Jesus feeds the five thousand and raises the dead, but I don't believe what I see for it may be the clever producers up to their tricks again!

The point is that you will not communicate faith to Fred by putting on a display of visuals. You should not address his eyes, but his ears. Faith comes by hearing, not seeing.

The promises of God can be verbalised either by being spoken aloud, and so heard, or by being written down, and so read. The Bible is one way (the best way) of reading the promises of God. 'These are written that you may believe that Jesus is the Christ, the Son of God, and that by believing you may have life in his name.'

Unwrapping the Bible in your neighbourhood

Guy lives in North Vancouver. The first time I met him was at a seminar I was teaching on how to introduce your neighbours to Jesus. The impression I formed was of a shy, awkward fellow with few social graces. But he was listening with rapt attention and went away full of excitement. 'Keep in touch,' I shouted after him, 'and let me know how you get on.'

He did keep in touch, in fact he phoned me several months later to report that he had developed the pattern of taking a daily walk around his neighbourhood, praying for the occupants by name. He had never actually met any of the people he was praying for. He was just too shy to talk to them, but he had done some research and drawn up a list of all their names.

The next time I met him was at Missionsfest, a huge conference in Vancouver. 'How are you making out in your neighbourhood, Guy?' I enquired.

He went bright red. 'I may have blown it,' he explained. Having prayed for each neighbour for six months, he felt constrained to take it a step further. He was too reserved to talk to anyone face to face, but he resolved to give them each a Bible. I imagined that he would buy a pack of cheap paperback versions with a cheerful cover. Not a bit of it. He was in the process of buying them each a genuine leather-bound edition, costing nearly $100 (£65) a time. 'That way they will value it all the more, and perhaps read it.'

'But however did you afford to buy twenty-five Bibles at $100 each?'

'Oh, I didn't buy them all at once. Each month I can afford two more Bibles, so I am working through the neighbourhood slowly, but I should have it all done within the year.'

'So why do you think you have blown it?'

He explained that he was too shy to give the Bibles to the people directly. He did it anonymously. He would wrap the Bible in strong protective brown paper and include a letter encouraging the people to read it. Then, under cover of darkness, he would leave it on their front doorstep. That had worked fine for the first few houses, but there was one house where the people were away on holiday when the Bible was delivered. When they arrived home, there on their doorstep was a suspicious package. They hadn't ordered anything. The postman would not have left it on the doorstep, nor would any respectable delivery service. It must be a bomb! So they called the police, who called the bomb squad, who evacuated the area and, using a long pole with a grab, gingerly lifted the package into the middle of the street, where they carefully, remotely and at huge expense to the tax payer, unwrapped a Bible!

Your own story illustrates the truth of God's promises

Simple testimony is the most convincing communication of all. For all his great wisdom, the apostle Paul used his testimony on at least three occasions, for three times it is recorded verbatim in the book of Acts. It's my guess that he must have trotted it out everywhere he went. When Billy Graham went to address the students and faculty of Cambridge University, he avoided intellectual arguments by simply telling the story of what God had done for him personally.

To what do you imagine Fred is most likely to respond? A potted sermon or a natural, personal testimonial from you, his friend? And what exactly is a testimony?

'Hey Fred! You'll never guess what happened yesterday! You know how my boss has been on my back about working overtime at weekends? And you know how concerned I was that this would interfere with my church responsibilities? Well, I have been praying about it, and just last night the boss called me into his office and said some nice things about my work and gave me a rise. He even said that he is hiring this new man so I needn't worry about the overtime!'

Over lunch: 'Fred, I read such a wonderful thing this morning. I try to read a page or two from the Bible every day and what I read today hit the spot. As you know, I have to go into hospital next week for a minor op. Of course, it is nothing to worry about, but sometimes . . . Well, here's what I read: "Fear not, for I have redeemed you; you are mine. When you pass through the waters, I will be with you; and when you pass through the rivers, they will not sweep over you. When you walk through the fire, you will not be burned; the flames will not set you ablaze. For I am the Lord, your God. You are precious and honoured in my sight, and I love you. Do not be afraid, for I am with you." That certainly cheers a body up!'

The Bible tells us always to be prepared to give an answer to everyone who asks us to give the reason for the hope that we have. So to toss out teasers along these lines is likely to precipitate just such a question: 'I can never quite figure this religion thing out. What is it with you and your church-going, anyway?' Now the way is open for you to tell just who Jesus is to you, how you came to faith, what he does for you day by day.

The beauty is that you don't have to be a rocket scientist to talk about your own experience of Jesus. Remember the healing of the blind man? Now that he has 20/20 vision, the authorities get hold of him and subject him to endless cross-examination. Finally they insist that the man has been fooled by Jesus, who must be a sinner of the worst order. I suppose the poor fellow could have launched into a homily on the nature of sin, the wages of sin, the forgiveness of sin and the confession of sin. He might have quoted from the original Hebrew and Greek. But he didn't. He merely responded. 'Whether he is a sinner or not, I don't know. One thing I do know. I was blind but now I see!' – personal testimony. End of argument!

Booklets summarise God's promises

However, Fred may need a more comprehensive picture of Jesus and his promises than those illustrated by your own experience. It is difficult to explain the facts of the faith in normal conversation. Unless you are exceptionally gifted, you may get all muddled. I have some clever friends who seem to have things so hammered down that they can communicate the vital facts all from memory. Most of us can't easily do that. But there are all sorts of helpful tools available to help us.

There are booklets such as *Peace with God*, by Billy Graham. The most widely used booklet of all is put out by Campus Crusade for Christ and is entitled: *The Four Spiritual Laws*. It is designed to be read aloud. They suggest that you sit down beside your friend so he can read along with you and look at the illustrations. It guides you through a conversation, asking the right questions and prompting the appropriate answers.

I have a friend who carries several copies of this booklet everywhere he goes. He went into the bank the other day to ask for a loan. Before the conversation was over he had produced his little book and taken the bank manager right through to the prayer at the end.

Another friend attended a Campus Crusade seminar on evangelism and how to use the *Four Spiritual Laws* booklet. She was told just what to do and that when you reached a certain point in the presentation the Holy Spirit would take over and the person would respond. Next day she went to visit a prisoner in a local jail, determined to put this idea to the test. She was a little put off because the prisoner she was visiting was not alone. Her cell mate was in the top bunk, listening to every word that was spoken. But despite her misgivings about its effectiveness, she pulled out her copy of the booklet. 'Have you ever heard of the four spiritual laws?'

'No, I can't say that I have.'

'Well, I have this little booklet which explains them. May I read it with you?'

'Carry on! I'm not going anywhere special.'

So she was away. She sat on the bed next to the prisoner with her cell mate in the bunk above listening to every word. It felt so mechanical and false. But when she came to the end, the part that gives a suggested prayer of acceptance of Jesus, she asked the question prompted by the script: 'Does this express the desire of your heart?'

'Yes, it does. I would like God to do that for me!'

'And so would I,' came a voice from the top bunk.

Booklets like that have been an invaluable help to place the promises of God before tens of thousands of people.

You can personalise this approach if you want to be creative. You can write something down and get it photocopied.

Writing a letter sets God's promises down on paper in your own words

I was asked by a lady whose marriage was falling

apart to meet her husband. He would not agree to marriage counselling and would not go to see the local pastor, but he did agree to meet me for three one-hour sessions.

We met at his place. I think I was as nervous as he was, sitting drinking coffee in his living-room.

'So what's the problem, Len?' I opened.

He told me. He was an insurance salesman and must have been equipped by the Blarney Stone for his job, for he never paused to take breath until the hour was up.

I went home feeling a failure. The conversation didn't go as I wanted. A week later, as I was praying in preparation for the second hour-long session, an idea struck me. I wrote him a letter. So when next we met, I jumped in fast, before he could get started. 'Len, you're a busy man and I don't want to waste your time. One hour is brief and we both want to make the very most of it. So I have taken the liberty of setting down in a letter the essential things that I want to share with you.'

I gave him the original and kept a copy myself. We read it through together, discussing each paragraph as we came to it. Here is how it ran:

Dear Len,

Knowing that our time together is short, I thought it might save us both time if I set down in letter form the heart of what I want to share with you. These are the essential facts that the Bible leads me to believe about you. (They are of course also true of me, but allow me to apply them personally to you in this letter.)

1 You are a deliberate, planned, purposeful creation of God. You didn't just happen. You are special.

2 God loves you and purposes for you your highest good. That purpose is that you should lovingly respect him, lovingly respect other people and lovingly respect yourself, and that therein you should be like God's own Son.

3 You have thus far lived largely outside that purpose. But God's love for you is as strong as ever and his purpose for you stands unaltered.

4 God has shown himself prepared to go to any lengths to re-secure your highest good. He has sent Jesus, his Son, to be on the receiving end of all the unloving disrespect that you (and the rest of us) could ever subject him to, and while at the lowest point to express his forgiveness. God showed that forgiveness had been accomplished by raising Jesus from death.

5 God's ultimate plan is to fulfil his purpose in you by placing the Holy Spirit of Jesus right in your body so that he can love through you.

6 God will never force on you his plan to restore you to his purpose. It is your prerogative to accept it in faith, or to reject it by neglect or outright refusal.

As a man accustomed to making a sale, you will realise that such an offer requires a close, and I would suggest that the day has come for you to make a definite response, positive or negative.
Yours sincerely

It worked like a charm! The letter set a framework

for our conversation. We had a handrail to follow, an agenda for our meeting. As we discussed each point I showed him where that was taught in the Bible and he raised such questions as he had. The final paragraph brought him right up to the need to act on what he had been told, to make a decision one way or the other. And Len did so. We knelt together beside his coffee table and he took a vital step towards Jesus.

High tech makes virtuous reality of God's promises

But there are many other ways of verbally communicating the promises of God so that Fred can hear them, choose them and believe them.

Is he a reader? Give him a book. After all, you're reading a book right now, so why wouldn't he?

Does Fred spend much time on the road? Well, give him a tape to listen to.

Video tapes are not so likely to get watched because TV tends to be a medium that demands your undivided attention. So why not invite him over to watch one with you? That way you get the added benefit of being able to talk over the content of the video when it's finished. Group watching is a great way of doing this. Recently our neighbourhood group rented a series of four 45-minute video lectures by Chuck Colson. Chuck has a great gift for straight talking. I couldn't say some of those things to a group of my friends sitting in my living-room. For a start I'm not clever enough, but even if I were, my friends might lynch me before I was finished. But if all I have to do is press the buttons and then let Chuck Colson do the talking, then we can all throw tomatoes together!

Small group discussions provide a forum for talking about God's promises

Perhaps the most natural environment to talk about Jesus in any neighbourhood is the context of a small group. When two or three neighbours meet in Jesus' name, inevitably they will talk about him.

In all the neighbourhood groups of which I have been a part, we have used the Bible as the agenda for our discussions. We follow a passage of Scripture, then we discuss it. I don't tell the group what I think the passage is saying to them. Sermons don't go down too well in neighbourhood groups. So we all sit under it and discuss how we can implement what it teaches. I have been to a few groups which follow the monologue style, where the leader pretends he is in the pulpit and lectures us for an hour. I hate that. It wastes the whole benefit of being in a small group. A church service is the time for that, or Sunday School.

If you have never been in a small group discussion, let me tell you how we operate and you can copy such ideas as may be helpful. The great advantage of this method is that it doesn't require much of the leader, either in the way of background knowledge or in advance preparation.

Happy tummies make relaxed neighbours

Mid-week gatherings tend to bring people a little stressed from their day at work, so time to chill out is vital. Refreshments at the end are OK, but at the beginning they are more useful. For a start they make people arrive on time, and then they help them to feel glad they came before getting down to business.

Explain what the evening is about

If it is a new group where neighbours are unused to prayer and Bible reading, then explain afresh the purpose of the evening – to help each other to become better parents, spouses, neighbours, citizens (whatever you want to stress!) with God's help. Assure them that no one will be put on the spot, called upon to pray out loud, sing an anthem or be embarrassed in any way. Tell them that the plan is to hold a discussion and to base it on a passage from the Bible. Then anyone who wants to can bring up any particular concerns, so that you can pray for God's help and lay plans for any appropriate action. Explain that no one there is an expert in the Bible or in prayer. You are all beginners, learning as you go along.

Provide Bibles

You would be wise to provide a stack of paperback Bibles on the assumption that some may not have their own. It is also helpful if everyone has the same translation and the same page numbering. For example, page 394 is much easier to find than 1 Chronicles chapter 29!

An easy pattern for Bible discussions

This is not intended to be a format, just a handrail that our group often uses. To make it more specific, let's base the outline on a specific Bible passage – John 2:1–11

1–2 On the third day a wedding took place at Cana in Galilee. Jesus' mother was there, and Jesus and his disciples had also been invited to the wedding.

3 When the wine was gone, Jesus' mother said to him, 'They have no more wine.'

4 'Dear woman, why do you involve me?' Jesus replied, 'My time has not yet come.'

5 His mother said to the servants, 'Do whatever he tells you.'

6 Nearby stood six stone water jars, the kind used by the Jews for ceremonial washing, each holding from twenty to thirty gallons.

7 Jesus said to the servants, 'Fill the jars with water'; so they filled them to the brim.

8–10 Then he told them, 'Now draw some out and take it to the master of the banquet.' They did so, and the master of the banquet tasted the water that had been turned into wine. He did not realise where it had come from, though the servants who had drawn the water knew. Then he called the bridegroom aside and said, 'Everyone brings out the choice wine first and then the cheaper wine after the guests have had too much to drink; but you have saved the best until now.'

11 This, the first of his miraculous signs, Jesus performed in Cana of Galilee. He thus revealed his glory, and his disciples put their faith in him.

First we pray that God will speak to us by the Holy Spirit through the passage to be studied. (If it is a group of people to whom this is all brand new, it may be a good idea to introduce the idea of praying later, when they are more relaxed. We don't want to blow them out of the water before we even open the Bible!)

Next we read the whole passage right through; in this case John 2:1–11. Sometimes we read it twice, just to make sure we have got it. It's good practice not to read round because some people, like me, are very poor readers, and to be put on the spot and expected to read out loud is a terrible embarrassment. So we ask someone to volunteer to read.

Then we discuss the passage, a paragraph at a time. The leader will re-read the specific section we are concentrating on, in this case verses 1–3 ('On the third day a wedding took place at Cana in Galilee. Jesus' mother was there, and Jesus and his disciples had also been invited to the wedding. When the wine was gone, Jesus' mother said to

him, "They have no more wine."'). Then he will
say: 'What kind of issues does this raise in your
experience? For example, can anyone identify with
the notion of running out of wine in a wedding, or
running out of love in a marriage?'

To begin with people may be a little hesitant to
open up. Making yourself vulnerable is the best way
of helping others to do so. But don't fall into the
trap of sermonising or even of talking too much.
Permit awkward silences to demand that one of your
neighbours should rescue you!

After discussion on that point is exhausted, the
leader will move the group on to the next paragraph, reading it out loud. '"Dear woman, why do
you involve me?" Jesus replied, "My time has not
yet come." His mother said to the servants, "Do
whatever he tells you." Now what bells does this
ring with you? Why did Mary involve Jesus? and
is there any value in involving Jesus in any of our
domestic difficulties? What would you guess Jesus
might tell us to do if we were to ask his advice?'

There is no vital need to reach the end of the
passage, so don't prolong it too much. Half an hour
is plenty and leaves people wanting more.

**At the end of the study time the leader asks
everyone to identify the main lesson** that he or she
has learned personally. Sometimes he also asks us
to say what we are going to do about implementing
that particular lesson. That is a little heavy and better
kept until people know each other better. But the
point is that it earths what might otherwise be just
an academic discussion.

Finally we turn our own main lesson into a

prayer. Anyone who wants to is invited to express to God a request that he will help them smarten up in that area. Or perhaps they will thank God for a fresh promise that seems to be just for them. Some may even express regret for past failures that the passage has brought back to their attention. But no one is made to feel awkward if they don't pray. Sometimes I deliberately refrain from praying just to make the other silent people feel OK.

This is a very unthreatening approach for people who are not used to this kind of thing. It leaves them free to take part or stay quiet. No one is preaching at anyone. The discussion has order, yet is open to debate. It leaves the door wide open for anyone to share a personal experience. But most importantly, it lays before each person present the promises of God so that all who hear them can believe them.

The Gospel of John builds faith in the neighbourhood

John's Gospel is perhaps the best book of the Bible on which to base a series of discussions for people who may not be sure of its truth. John wrote it 'that you may believe that Jesus is the Christ, the Son of God, and that by believing you may have life in his name'. Just exactly what Fred needs.

And it was for that very reason that Brian and Dianne Dahl used John as their outline for their first stab at forming a neighbourhood group. They let it be known that they were planning to host a series of ten discussions based on the Gospel of John from the Bible. No previous knowledge of the Bible would be necessary and people with any faith or none would be equally welcome. A dozen people responded to the invitation, encouraged by the thought that it was just for ten weeks rather than an open-ended commitment.

It was the third week when they studied the story of Nicodemus in John chapter 3. It included that famous verse about God loving the world so much that he gave his only Son, Jesus, so that whoever should believe in him would not perish, but instead would live for ever. That verse went over big! Faith came by hearing and faith came in spades. Everyone present heard the promise of God. The promise of life by believing in Jesus was so attractive that they all hoped for it, even though they could not see it. And faith grabbed hold of it and became a sure thing, a certainty.

In the prayer time at the end, John and Margaret from up the road were so overcome they could hardly speak. John managed to pray that somehow they would be able to pass this beautiful thing on to their family and friends.

On the way home, a short walk up the street, John and Margaret passed Alex, a neighbour who had just finished washing his car. 'Nice evening for a stroll,' he called.

'We've just been down at Brian and Dianne's place for the evening.'

'Oh, did they have a party or something? I noticed a few cars in their driveway.'

'Not a party, no. It was a discussion based on the Bible.'

'That's nice.' Alex sounded a little non-committal. 'What sort of thing did you discuss?'

'Oh, you wouldn't believe what we got into tonight. It was wonderful. You know that famous verse that people display on banners at sporting events – John 3:16? Well, we discussed that. We never realised that having everlasting life was a gift God gave to people who trusted Jesus. We always thought it was a reward for being religious, but in fact anyone can have it, even ordinary people like ourselves.'

Alex poured the water from his bucket into the gutter beside the road and wrung out his sponge. The hard drive in his brain was whirring. 'You two wouldn't like to come in for a drink, would you? I'd love to hear more about all this.' The conversation went on until 12.15. During that time Alex and his wife heard the promise of God. They too found it attractive and the faith to grab hold of it began to form. Faith was coming by hearing . . .

When eventually John and Margaret got home the phone was ringing. 'Who can that be at this time of night?' they wondered. It was their son. 'Where have you been? I've been calling and calling. I thought something terrible must have happened. You are never out this late. Where were you?'

'We were at a neighbourhood discussion.'

'Whatever were you discussing until gone midnight?'

'Well, as a matter of fact we were discussing the most famous verse in the Bible . . .' Margaret passed

on to her son the words of the promise. The son heard
it. Was it the beginnings of faith that caused him to
respond: 'That's cool!'

Preachers are God's special gift to verbalise God's promises

Another way you can communicate the promises of
God to Fred is by inviting him to hear a preacher
proclaim Jesus. But I fear that in some places the
evangelist is in bad odour with the Church and the
world alike.

My wife Joy, who is a nurse, was giving a pill to
a patient the other Sunday. He was watching TV,
where a well-known televangelist was weeping and
sobbing in his attempt to raise funds for his ministry.
'What a load of garbage!' muttered the patient.

'Yes, well, I have to agree that I too find it
offensive. But among all the garbage is treasure.
That chap is expressing some of the most precious
truths that have ever been heard. But the manner
of his presentation makes the whole thing appear
unacceptable.'

At a recent worldwide congress on evangelism,
one lady argued that the role of the evangelist is
currently obsolete! But the role of the evangelist is
to so express the Lord Jesus that people may believe
who he is, trust what he has done and accept what
he promises. Is that an obsolete role? God forbid!

In Canada, where I live, there are very few full-
time preaching evangelists, just a handful of people
whose primary role is to speak to the 90 per cent

of the population who are not yet Christians. There must be tens of thousands of full-time workers who are pastors or teachers and whose primary role is to address the 10 per cent who already are Christians. Something is badly wrong.

We did a tour of Canadian Bible schools and theological colleges a year or so back, the object of which was to encourage students to become evangelists. In almost every school we visited we put to the student body the question: 'How many of you are planning to be pastors?' Dozens of hands would rise. 'How many teachers?' Again a good showing. 'And overseas missionaries?' Fewer hands, but quite respectable. 'How many of you are planning to become full-time evangelists working in this country?' We hardly ever saw a hand.

When we asked them why they felt no call to be evangelists they confessed that they found the role of the evangelist to be unattractive or unattainable. 'After all, who could ever be like Billy Graham and who would want to be like Jimmy What's-his-name?' We discovered that almost all students had a mental image of an evangelist as being a sweating, loud-mouthed, motivational speaker, with white suit and shoes, a TV ministry and a dubious private life. They suspected him of money-grubbing and equated him with a used car salesman.

So when I suggest taking Fred to hear a preacher proclaim Jesus, someone may well flip on to the next chapter or change the channel. But hang on a minute! Not all preachers are the same. God has given some wonderful communicators to the Church. Some of them are big names, but most are nobodies.

Some are official 'Evangelists', but most are pastors, businessmen and women, construction workers, just ordinary people who are gifted to be spokespersons of the gospel.

Ken and Linda live in Vancouver, in a moderate house overlooking a ravine. They have lived there for twelve years and are well-established members of the neighbourhood. No one could fail to recognise that they are religious, yet they are good neighbours, friendly and fun to know.

Last year they persuaded Terry Winter, a nationally known evangelist with a widely watched TV show, to come to their home to address a neighbourhood gathering. When they had a date nailed down, Ken and Linda went to work to persuade as many of their neighbours as possible to attend. They printed special cards in the hope that if the invitation was seen to be serious, then the response might be likewise. The event was billed as a neighbourhood dinner party with special guest 'the well-known TV personality Terry Winter, who will talk about his faith in the context of modern Canadian society'.

The initial reaction of many was to decline so direct an approach. However, Ken and Linda had invested twelve years in that neighbourhood and many of those neighbours owed them. It was time to call in the debts! It must have cost Ken and Linda dearly, for they risked many friendships and even their good standing in the neighbourhood. But when the night came they packed in a house full of neighbours. Joy and I were there to give a hand. They had removed all the furniture from their living-room and dining area and had borrowed round tables and chairs from their church. The whole place was transformed into a cosy restaurant, with beautifully laid table settings and candles on the tables. We were surprised to see how free Ken and Linda were to mingle with the guests, until we realised that the catering was all being taken care of by discreet members of their church.

The meal was superb and conversation flowed ever more freely as the guests relaxed. Ken and Linda are abstainers, but they were wise enough to permit a couple of good quality bottles of wine on the side for those who chose to drink alcohol. When all the dishes were cleared, Ken stood up and welcomed everyone and introduced Terry.

What followed was a winsome, inoffensive, yet direct proclamation of Jesus: who he is, what he has done and what he promises to do for each person who will trust him. Every person present heard. And as faith comes by hearing, faith was born in the hearts of some, while unavoidably others scoffed, politely of course, for it was a wonderful dinner party!

Without faith it is impossible to please God, because anyone who comes to him must believe that he exists and that he rewards those who earnestly seek him.

If Fred is to please God, he must first believe that he exists. Faith comes by hearing. So hear Fred must.

13

Breaking the Deadlock

Forgiving in Jesus' name brings reconciliation

He told them, '. . . repentance and forgiveness of sins will be preached in his name to all nations, beginning at Jerusalem'.

Repent . . . every one of you, in the name of Jesus Christ for the forgiveness of your sins.

It was with a terrible sense of inadequacy that I drove into the driveway, parked the car and forced myself to walk up to the front door. I was deliberately half an hour early for the appointment because I wanted to spend some time with Arnold before Darlene arrived. He answered my knock immediately, pathetically glad to see me.

'Do you want a cup of tea?' he enquired.

How could I refuse such an offer from a fellow British Canadian?

'Sit down, won't you.' It was hard to find a place to sit. Half the furniture had gone from what a few weeks previously had been a lovely home. The few remaining chairs were festooned with unironed laundry. Arnold brought the tea with an apology. 'Sorry! No milk.' I hate canned milk in tea, but I pretended to like it.

'Justyn, I don't know how I am going to face this. I haven't seen Darlene since she left. We have tried to talk on the phone a few times, but it always ends in a fight. A couple of times when I called a man answered the phone. I hung up straight away. I guess it was this Carlos fellow. How could she do this to me?'

Arnold and Darlene had parted company a month previously. She had left, taking with her the two children, both under five. Next day, while Arnold was out looking for work, a van had arrived and taken half the furniture.

I had been to see Darlene. She explained that she could no longer tolerate Arnold's irresponsibility. 'Justyn, you know that he can never hold a job for longer than a few weeks. Then he spiritualises it, saying that it must be the Lord's will, or something. We are up to our ears in debt, behind on the mortgage and all he says is: "The Lord will provide"! But he never gets off his backside to do anything about it. I just can't take it any more. I can cope better on my own without him hanging round my neck.'

Finally they had agreed to sit down together to discuss the situation and they had asked me to be there to see fair play.

The door rattled as a key refused to throw

the catch, then the door bell chimed. Arnold had changed the locks. He went white, got up and opened the door. Two little children erupted eagerly into the hall, glad to be back in their familiar home. Darlene followed, and behind her a stranger who looked as if he was from central America.

'This is Carlos,' she announced. 'Do you object if he sits in on this?'

I knew Arnold did object with every ounce of his being. I was there as a mediator so I leapt in. 'Darlene, it might be better if we had a chance to talk first with just you and Arnold alone.' She opened her mouth to argue, so I turned to Carlos, grabbed his hand and shook it. 'You don't mind waiting out in the car for a few minutes, do you?' He mumbled an acceptance in a thick Spanish accent and was gone.

More unpalatable tea was poured while attention was directed to the children as they ran round the house. This was not going to be easy.

Then television came to the rescue and the children were switched into neutral as they sat on the floor, anaesthetised from the real world, a once safe world that was now falling apart while they watched Big Bird.

'My dears,' I started. 'There is something very special at stake here. Not just your own happiness and rights, but those of the children too. We must find a way of solving this.'

Darlene was first out of the blocks. 'Justyn, I have lived with Arnold for six years. It was fine to begin with, but bit by bit we have grown apart. I just don't love him any more.'

'Well, I still love you, Darlene.'

'How can you say you love me when you do nothing to provide for me?'

'I have tried, Darlene. No one can do better than try his hardest. And anyway, I have an interview tomorrow for this super job . . .'

'Always tomorrow, Arnold. Always another interview, another idea, another business enterprise. When will you get real?'

'It's not a matter of getting real. The Lord will come up with something—'

'Baloney!' This was too much for Darlene. 'Arnold, why don't you stop hiding behind your religion and take some responsibility? God helps those who help themselves. It's your irresponsible attitude that has destroyed our marriage.'

'Oh! So it's my fault, is it? And what about that fellow sitting out there in the car. I suppose he is my fault. Are you sleeping with him?'

'And what if I were?'

The debate went on for perhaps half an hour. Mine was supposed to be the ministry of reconciliation. It was all I could do to avoid bloodshed. Finally Darlene stormed out, dragging the bewildered children with her. A year later they were divorced.

There is nothing unusual about the incident. It is re-enacted daily in countless disintegrating families, but it illustrates something vital about the introduction of Fred to Jesus. And it's this . . .

Jesus and Fred are incompatible!

Fred has accepted a lifestyle which he enjoys

and justifies as the way he is. Jesus is holy, absolutely pure and sinless. To him, Fred's lifestyle is anathema. As Arnold cannot accept Carlos and Darlene cannot accept Arnold's sloth, much more can Jesus not accept Fred's sin. And how does Fred view Jesus' holiness? I doubt whether he can see past a bunch of prohibitions: 'Don't do this. Don't touch that.'

So as you sit down with Jesus on the one hand and Fred on the other, seeking to make the introduction, you are entrusted by God with the ministry of reconciliation. You are therefore Christ's ambassador, as though God were making his appeal through you. 'We implore you (Fred). Be reconciled to God.'

Make no mistake about it, you have a difficult task. It is not as though you were seeking to introduce two rather nice, like-minded people with mutual interests. Sin and holiness are as far apart as are light and darkness. The two are mutually exclusive and cannot mix.

So who is going to bend? In the example of Arnold and Darlene both were in the wrong and both needed to bend. But between Fred and Jesus that is not the case. Jesus is absolutely in the right. He does not need to justify his position, for he is utterly good. There is no way he is going to bend in compromise to walk in friendship with Fred down sinful avenues. And there is no way that Jesus is going to concede that maybe holiness is a little extreme and asking a bit too much of any man. Perhaps Fred has got a point and if Fred is willing to start being a little more religious, then, just maybe, Jesus will become a little less perfect!

Though God invites Fred to reason with him, 'Come let us reason together', he does not invite Fred to negotiate, to seek a compromise solution. 'Though your sins are like scarlet, they shall be as white as snow; though they are red as crimson, they shall be like wool.' Jesus is certainly not going to join Fred in his sinfulness, but neither is he prepared to meet on middle ground, in the grey area somewhere between sin and righteousness. Jesus is determined to cause Fred to share his holiness. He has nothing less in mind for Fred than perfection.

So how does Fred feel about that? Does he warm to the idea of becoming holy? Is he ready to confess himself a sinner and renounce his former life? Or does he seek to justify himself, arguing that he is not a sinner or, at least, no worse a sinner than everybody else?

It looks a lot like deadlock to me.

To make it worse, there is an ultimatum laid down by one party. 'I tell you the truth, unless you change . . . you will never enter the kingdom of heaven . . . The wages of sin is death.'

It's hard to foster friendship between two people you are seeking to introduce to each other when the one demands that the other change or die. Neither Arnold nor Darlene was prepared to accept the position of the other. They both demanded that the other change. Leave Carlos! Get a permanent job! . . . or face the consequences – divorce. Similarly Jesus says to Fred: 'Repent or die.' Fred says to Jesus: 'Accept me as I am, or forget it.'

Who will break the deadlock?

You are the mediator, the one entrusted with the task of reconciliation. Can you more readily persuade Fred to become holy or Jesus to become sin?

Forget it! You are too late to do either, for the initiative has already been taken. God made Jesus who had no sin to be sin for Fred, so that in him Fred might become the righteousness of God. Jesus became utterly sinful so that Fred might become utterly holy.

Jesus is not sitting in remote holiness waiting for Fred to shape up and repent before he will even look at him. God demonstrates his own love for Fred in this: while Fred was still a sinner, Christ died for Fred. When Fred was God's enemy, he was reconciled to God through the death of Jesus.

If, therefore, God has taken such an initiative to bring reconciliation, what remains for Fred to do? Quite simply, to respond. Repentance is not the cause of God's forgiveness, but rather a response to it. It is not the impressive nature of Fred's repentance which will persuade God to forgive him, it is the immensity of God's forgiveness that will persuade Fred to repent. It is God's kindness which leads us to repentance.

The job of Ambassador for Reconciliation is a two-fold appeal

There is no way to side-step this issue. Sooner

or later as you continue the introduction between Jesus and Fred, Fred will become aware of the difference between him and Jesus. Then he will have to choose. 'Do I want to walk with Jesus along the path towards holiness, or do I want to continue to go my own way?'

Your job, should you accept it, is the God-given ministry of reconciliation. You make your appeal to Fred: 'Fred, I implore you on Christ's behalf, be reconciled to God.' And you make your appeal to God: 'God, I implore you in Jesus' name, be merciful to Fred.'

In order to be successful in making the introduction of Fred to Jesus, you must be successful in the above appeals, to Fred on the one hand and to God on the other. The role of Ambassador for Reconciliation is the role of the intercessor who puts himself in the firing line of both sides of the argument and risks taking a bullet both ways. It is not a comfortable position to be in.

Consider the second appeal first.

God, be merciful to Fred!

A year or two back a number of Christians living in Vancouver felt that God was telling them of an impending earthquake that would devastate the city and cause tidal waves that would drown those who survived the initial shock. They even predicted the date when this would occur. So convinced were they that they paid for space in the local paper to warn people. As the day drew near there was a flurry of street preaching, warning people to flee from the wrath to come. Some argued that God was justified in his judgment and people were at last to receive their just desserts.

Minibus-loads of Christians got out of town, heading for high ground and open country. The day came and went – and nothing happened. Minibus-loads of embarrassed Christians came back into town.

The question of the wisdom or otherwise of those who published this 'prophecy' is not the issue I am raising here. But the incident illustrates an important point. Suppose God really did warn the population of a city of coming judgment, just as he warned Nineveh through Jonah. What would be the appropriate way to make your appeal to God on behalf of your friends?

Should you warn them and then get out of town? How would Fred have felt if you had warned him of the danger and then waved him goodbye as you drove off up the street with a minibus-load of hymn-singing friends? How would God have felt as he heard your hymns and watched you drive away from Fred to safety? How did God feel about Jonah as he took his grandstand seat on a hill to witness the destruction of Nineveh?

But suppose you acted differently. You delivered the warning which Fred didn't take seriously. So instead of driving off to save your own skin, you drove down to the sea wall. There you took your stance in the very place where the tidal wave would first hit. And there you made your appeal to God: 'God, for Jesus' sake, be merciful to Fred! He is no worse a sinner than I am, in fact he is a better person than me. He does not yet know the truth and it is I who am responsible for that. Will you destroy Fred for his ignorance? If anyone deserves death it is not Fred but me. So if you are going to bring destruction on this city, you will have to destroy me first. You destroy Fred over my dead body!'

From which position would you make the more convincing appeal: from the safety of the top of a mountain or the peril of the sea wall? Where would God be pleased to find you?

Over my dead body!

The point is that a vital part of the introduction of our neighbour to Jesus is the reality of the coming judgment of God. If Fred doesn't change, if he doesn't repent, he faces the sharp end of God's displeasure. Where do you stand in this issue? 'Well, God, I have put into practice all that I have learned in the first few chapters of *Love Your Neighbour for God's Sake* and Fred is just not interested. I know that you will one day judge all men and when you do I'll go to heaven and Fred will go to hell. Pity, but there is nothing more I can do!' Or do you argue: 'I know that one day you will judge all men, but if you are planning death for Fred, then kill me first!'?

Well, doesn't the Bible teach that all believers will go to heaven and all unbelievers will go to hell? Should we not simply agree with God that his judgments are just and his wrath is unavoidable? I don't think so.

Paul didn't just lie down and accept the coming annihilation of his neighbourhood as inevitable. He argued: 'For I could wish that I myself were cursed and cut off from Christ for the sake of my brothers, those of my own race.'

And neither did Moses. When the Israelites built a golden calf and worshipped it, God was set to wipe them off the face of the earth, starting afresh with Moses as the father of his new chosen people. Do you think Moses said: 'Oh, good idea, God. This is only justice, after all. Let them all die in the hell of your judgment while I enjoy the heaven of your approval.' Not a bit of it. He climbed up the mountain and stood before God and made his appeal: 'Oh, what a great sin these people have committed! They have made themselves gods of gold. But now, please forgive their sin – but if not, then blot me out of the book you have written.' That was pretty close to saying: 'Destroy them over my dead body!'

Later, when the Israelites complained against the leadership of Moses and Aaron, the Lord sent a plague that swept through the assembled multitude like a wave moving across a lake. Instead of standing by, watching the people receive harsh justice, Aaron rushed into the crowd and stood where the wave would reach next. He stood between the living and the dead and the plague stopped. By standing there his appeal was far more eloquent than it would have been from the sidelines. 'The next person to die is me, God. Over my dead body will this plague continue.'

King David sinned in that he ordered the people of his kingdom to be counted. But God had promised

Abraham that they would be as uncountable as the grains of sand on the seashore and as innumerable as the stars of heaven. Was it because David didn't trust God's promise that he ordered the uncountable to be counted? Abraham had trusted to the point that when his descendants had numbered only one – his son Isaac – he had been willing to sacrifice him to God on Mount Moriah, confident that God would still be capable of keeping his promise. But David, who by then had millions of subjects, insisted on counting them so he could measure his human resources.

So displeased was God with David's unbelief that he sent a destroying angel throughout the nation to make a nonsense of David's census. Thousands died. Finally the angel came to the outskirts of Jerusalem and hovered above the top of that same Mount Moriah where Abraham had nearly offered Isaac. His eyes were ablaze with the wrath of God against sin and his blood-dripping sword pointed towards the city. That is where David met him.

David walked forward to where the very tip of the sword was pointing at his own throat and made his appeal to God: 'I am the one who has sinned and done wrong. These are but sheep. What have they done? O Lord my God, let your hand fall upon me and my family, but do not let this plague remain on your people' – over my dead body will you touch this city! The plague was stopped.

And that became the very site upon which the Temple was built. For the place of intercession is the place where God chooses to be worshipped.

Years later Jesus walked on to that same mountain, now crowned by the half-rebuilt Temple. He saw

nothing but a market, offerings, fund-raising, building extensions and proliferation of programmes. He
saw the thermometer on the Temple wall measuring
the resources of the building fund, much as David's
census had sought to measure the resources of
his men. He cried aloud: 'Is it not written: "My
house will be called a house of prayer for all
nations"? But you have made it a den of robbers.' Heart-broken that religious people were com-
placently building the walls of protection for their
superiority, Jesus became sin, putting himself on
the sharp end of God's judgment. Suspended by
nails from a cross, Jesus interceded: 'Father, forgive them!' – over my dead body will they suffer hell.

So was God pleased with Moses, Aaron, David
and Jesus, all of whom put themselves in the very
place where God had promised hell and judgment, effectively sacrificing their own position of
safety and comfort? You can bet your life he
was!

God told the Israelites: 'I looked for a man among
them who would build up the wall and stand before
me in the gap on behalf of the land so that I would
not have to destroy it.'

So how will you make your appeal to God on
behalf of Fred? From a safe position of guaranteed
heaven, or standing self-sacrificially in the gates
of hell?

But what of the other side of the appeal, the appeal
to Fred?

Fred, be reconciled to God!

How can I most effectively make my appeal to Fred? Do I have to convince him that he is a sinner who must turn or burn?

An old Irish evangelist once ran through the streets of the city ringing a bell and shouting, 'Fire! Fire!' A crowd quickly gathered in alarm, demanding to know where the fire was. 'It's the fire of hell and if you don't repent, you'll all burn in it!'

My sister led me to Jesus as a child. She drew my attention to an old Victorian picture depicting the broad way that leads to destruction and the narrow way that leads to life. She pointed to hell and told me: 'That's where you're going because you're not a Christian!' I was so terrified that I accepted Jesus soon after.

But I wouldn't recommend that as a helpful way of introducing your neighbour to Jesus. Jesus didn't use such scare tactics. Yes, he spoke of hell, but always to motivate believers away from complacency, never to motivate unbelievers away from hell.

But is there then no place for warning people to flee from the wrath to come? Yes, there most certainly is. For there is much of that in the Bible. Ezekiel paints a very vivid picture of a watchman who, knowing that the enemy was coming, kept silent. He would be held responsible for the slaughter which would follow. He should have given clear warning of the impending disaster.

Using the coming judgment to motivate neighbours to be reconciled to God

Jill was devastated when her husband had left her to shack up with another woman. The whole experience led her to seek God and she started to attend our church. We got to know her quite well. We saw her struggling to bring up her two small children alone, scrimping and saving just to keep food on the table, working all day at a minimum wage and studying all evening to better her earning potential. It made me mad.

'Justyn, would you go and see Rob and perhaps talk some sense into him?' I agreed to go.

I was nervous at confronting a stranger, but mad as hell, which kept me going. I arrived at the address. There was a gleaming Harley Davidson parked in the car port. Oh no! Not a biker!

The bell didn't work so I knocked. I could hear rock music doing its thing, but no one stirred. There was probably no one in, so I banged until my knuckles hurt. That made me feel better and it also produced a response. A cursing and a muttering drew nearer. The door opened, and there in just a pair of tattered jeans stood a seven-foot biker, tattoos, hair, the whole bit. 'Whaaaddddyouuwant?'

'Are you Rob King?'

'Who wants to know?'

'I'm Justyn Rees and I'm a minister at the Community Bible Church and a friend of your wife Jill.'

'So?'

'I'd like to talk to you. May I come in?'

I sat amid the empty beer bottles and tried to get down to what I wanted to say above the noise of the radio, which Rob showed little sign of turning down. At that moment a girl in a dressing-gown shuffled into the room and killed the noise. 'Who are you?' she asked me.

'Justyn. I'm a preacher.'

'So why are you here?' asked Rob morosely.

'Rob, you have abandoned your wife and two children and are living immorally with another woman. I am here to ask what you are going to do about it.'

Now that's not the kind of small talk that you expect to encounter from a total stranger sitting in your own living-room when you have just got out of bed. So taken aback was he that he didn't hit me. 'I'd say that was none of your goddam business!' was all he managed.

'You could be right there. But it is Jill's business and little Lucy's and Craig's. You are wronging them deeply.'

No response.

'And another thing. It is God's business. He always champions the cause of anyone who suffers injustice. Rob, you may be able to ignore Jill and the children. You can also tell me it is none of my business, but God will hold you accountable and one day soon you will have to answer to him!'

He went white, then mumbled: 'Would you like a coffee or something?' The girl shuffled off and poured black liquid into a filthy mug.

We talked for some time. Be sure he justified his actions. There are always two sides to every dispute. But his chief line of defence was his refusal to acknowledge my God as the only god. 'I believe in my higher power. But I don't go along with the Ten Commandments and all that crap.'

My parting challenge to Rob was for him to accompany me to a Billy Graham crusade meeting the following week. To my amazement he agreed. No, he didn't respond to the invitation. No, he was not terribly impressed. No, he did not become a Christian. But he did invite me to attend his AA meeting, which I did, and I was impressed, deeply impressed.

A level playing field with no dividing walls

What moved me was the experience of a bunch of people who made no pretence of perfection, people who were unanimously open about their problem. Each speaker prefaced their comments by confessing themselves to be an alcoholic. Every person present wanted to be dry, but every one of them had a common problem.

The place where we Christians find ourselves caught is somewhere between being a faithful watchman who warns of the coming judgment of God against sin, and being the Pharisee who is itching to stone a sinner to death with Bible texts.

When the woman caught in the very act of adultery was dragged by her accusers before Jesus for his judgment in the matter, she quickly found that the safest place for her was as close a possible to a holy Jesus and as far as possible from the sinful religious people around her.

It bothers me that people outside the Church have formed the opinion that we Christians are stone-throwers, accusing everybody outside our number of being sinners and threatening them with hell. Yet at the same time we cannot water down what the Bible so clearly teaches in order to make the message more palatable. So what can we do?

I once interviewed Malcolm Muggeridge, the journalist cynic turned Christian. The interview took place not long after he had found faith and many Christians were as hesitant to accept him into the fold as had been the early Church to accept the newly converted Paul. When we opened the interview to general questions from the floor, one gentleman asked: 'Mr Muggeridge, are you certain that you have everlasting life?'

The old man paused, then peeping out from under his bushy white eyebrows he said slowly, 'I hope so.'

'Yes, but are you sure?' his questioner persisted.

'How could one so unworthy as I presume to be sure of so wonderful a salvation?'

'Because God's word promises it!'

'Yes, and I believe the Bible. But I am still overwhelmed with my own unworthiness.'

I fear that so glib and self-assured are we of our forgiveness, our right standing as children of God, our guarantee of heaven when we die, that we distance ourselves from others who don't share our faith. Of course we are right to be assured of these things, but are we right to use them to build fresh barriers between us and the rest of the world?

'I am a Christian and you are a non-Christian.'

'I am forgiven; you are a sinner.'

'I am a child of God; you are under his condemnation.'

'I am going to heaven when I die; you are going to hell.'

Did Jesus build these barriers or did Jesus come to break down the barriers and the dividing walls of hostility?

But while we cannot pretend that everyone will be saved and that there is no hell, we can at least acknowledge ourselves to be sinners. What I so appreciated about Rob's AA meeting was that there were no alcoholics and non-alcoholics. Each speaker who stood up started his testimony by saying: 'I'm John and I'm an alcoholic.' No one said: 'I'm John and I used to be an alcoholic.' Consequently there were no barriers. Everyone was in the same boat, beggars telling other beggars where to get bread.

Transpose that atmosphere to a church meeting. Someone stands up to give a testimony: 'I'm John and I used to be a sinner. Now I am a born-again Christian saved by grace. And I just want to tell all you non-Christians who are here tonight . . .' Barriers, barriers! Us and them! Holier than thou!

If every person giving testimony, every preacher standing up in the pulpit, could start by assuring his listeners that we are all level pegging, all sinners, all needing repentance, all needing faith in his promises, all undeserving of his kindness and of heaven, then we would be in a better position to make our appeal to our friends. Instead of shouting down from the lofty superiority of our pedestal of assurance, we could be beggars telling other beggars where to get bread. Penitent sinners lead more people to Jesus than assured saints.

Am I suggesting that we abandon our assurance of God's promises and feign uncertainty in order to be more user-friendly? No, but I am saying that repentance and faith are not once-for-all acts. They are ongoing. Repentance is not something I did as a child and need never repeat. I have sinned today. I am still a sinner. I am not satisfied to sit down under that, so I repent of it. I turn every moment from my selfishness and failure to God's promises and forgiveness. I am more aware now of my sinfulness and unworthiness of God's friendship than ever I was as a child asking Jesus into my heart for the first time. Neither is faith something I once attained like passing an examination, a hurdle which, once jumped, need never be crossed again. I still grapple with trusting God's promises. This very day I am faced with insufficient funds to pay the mortgage, and the promise of God to supply all my needs. Should I trust or should I quit my work as an evangelist and pursue a more lucrative career?

My testimony is therefore: 'I'm Justyn and I'm a sinner. I am here to repent of my sins and to trust his promise of forgiveness. If anyone is interested in joining me, let's do it together!'

God be merciful to me, a sinner!

So, to be practical, how can we make our appeal to Fred in such a way as to lead him to repentance towards God?

It starts with me and my own personal attitude. I need to develop the mentality of 'God be merciful to me, a sinner' rather than 'I thank you, O God, that I am not as other men!' And I need to reflect that in the way I relate to Fred.

'Fred. You know I really admire you in the way you are so helpful to the people around you. Nothing seems to be too much trouble for you. I'm a preacher and am always talking about loving your neighbour, but you are so much better at actually doing it than I am. Would you help me? Where do I go wrong?'

'Fred, I sat up late last night and watched this really unpleasant movie. Why I didn't get off my backside and turn it off, I really don't know. But now it plays over and over in my mind. I feel polluted. How do you cope with that kind of thing?'

'Fred, I am so sorry that I snapped at you yesterday. I have been under a lot of pressure lately from the boss and I don't know what got into me. Please would you forgive me?'

'Fred, I met such an interesting person at church over the weekend. He was a Hell's Angel and a really violent person. But he told me that he met Jesus in prison and became a Christian, and it has made such a difference to him. He seemed a true gentleman. I would love God to do that for me more and more.'

This is not putting on an act for Fred's benefit. In fact rather the opposite. This is life. This is how I am. If I seek to hide it from Fred and put on an impressive facade of righteousness then I won't fool Fred anyway and will probably build a barrier between him and me. But if I can honestly show Fred my real self, struggling on the ropes of sin, discontented with my selfishness and determined to turn from it to God, then he may take my hand and follow.

A General Confession

And repentance is an attitude that we need to model as a Church. I was brought up an Anglican, attended an Anglican school and have a great love of the reverence that is expressed in the Anglican liturgy. There is something very stirring about being part of a congregation on its knees before God saying:

Almighty and most merciful Father, We have erred and strayed from thy ways like lost sheep. We have followed too much the devices and desires of our own hearts. We have offended against thy holy laws. We have left undone those things which we ought to have done, And we have done those things which we ought not to have done, And there is no health in us. But thou, O Lord, have mercy upon us, miserable offenders. Spare thou them, O God, which confess their faults. Restore thou them that are penitent, According to thy promises

declared unto mankind in Christ Jesus, our
Lord. And grant, O most merciful Father, for
his sake, that we may hereafter live a godly,
righteous and sober life, to the glory of thy
holy Name.

If Fred found himself in the company of a large
group of people who were expressing repentance,
it could encourage him to join them. But it could
be a stumbling block to him if he were to be singled
out, along with a few other unsuspecting individuals
who were hiding out in the congregation, as the only
sinner present who needed to make a spectacle of
himself by coming to the front in public repentance.
I am not suggesting that we should replace altar
calls with the General Confession. I am saying that
a penitent congregation can do more to lead others
in repentance than can a smug, assuredly righteous
congregation.

The path to revival has always been beaten by the repentant

Repentance has always been the hallmark of genuine
revival. In the 1700s George Whitfield, John Wesley
and others led the way in revival. For Wesley it all
started long after he was an ordained clergyman. He
had served as a missionary in Georgia and returned
to England a broken and disillusioned man. In a
small meeting hall in Aldersgate Street he felt his
heart strangely warmed. Thereafter people were
broken in deep conviction of sin everywhere he

went. People would fall to the floor and writhe in an agony of horror for their guilt until Wesley prayed for their forgiveness and release. The movement was typified by a definite turning from sin to holiness.

During the revivals in western Scotland there were similar manifestations of repentance. The Spirit of God would sweep over the hills like wind through the heather. Men would fall smitten by their consciousness of sin. Again it was the religious churchgoers who led the way in repentance. If God's judgment is to begin with the household of God, so must repentance.

In Saskatoon, Saskatchewan, in the early 1970s Lou and Ralph Sutera were booked to conduct a series of meetings in the Ebenezer Baptist Church. One hundred and sixty-five people were present for the opening night. No one responded to the invitation. The next night was similarly unspectacular. But a Sunday School teacher who was also a deaconess confessed her selfish, critical spirit. It must have been this lady who beat the path of repentance for others to follow. Her husband was next, and soon after came his brother, with whom he had not been on speaking terms for years.

The numbers of people confessing themselves to be sinners and repenting grew nightly until the meeting outgrew the Ebenezer Baptist Church and the crusade had to be moved to the Anglican church.

The pastor of the Christian and Missionary Alliance Church was sceptical about the crusade and planned to keep his people at home by organising a rival series of meetings. But it was hard to ignore what was happening up the road. He reluctantly cancelled their own meetings and allowed his flock to join the Sutera crusade. He himself attended and sat sceptically in the balcony. The preaching was nothing to write home about. The soloist was off key. The person giving testimony had nothing worthwhile to share. But at the close of the meeting, so convicted was he of the dry barrenness of his own ministry that he went forward to confess himself in need of God's forgiveness. Next day, at a pastors' meeting, he confessed his party spirit and selfish ambitions and led the way of repentance for his fellow church ministers.

Those meetings, which often lasted all through the night, were characterised by deep repentance. The crusade was extended and lasted for weeks and the repercussions of what happened there spread all over the country and beyond.

The point is that we can better help our friends to repent by leading them than by pushing them.

Repentance is not a performance

Expressions of repentance such as I have suggested are not merely for Fred's benefit. I am not suggesting that if Christian people model repentance, others will follow their lead, going through the outward appearance of repentance. No. The motions and words of repentance are not repentance at all if they are not the genuine expression of the heart. If they are a show, a demonstration for Fred's benefit, then they are certainly not a cry to the Almighty: 'God, be merciful to me, a sinner.' Neither do the motions and words of repentance oblige the Holy Spirit to bring heartfelt conviction of sin, which will cause genuine repentance. The examples history gives us of real revival are men going through the motions and saying the words of repentance from the heart, *in response* to the conviction of the Holy Spirit.

O Holy Spirit of God, convict me of sin that I may lead others in genuine repentance. Let me say with David, in all sincerity:

> I know my transgressions, and my sin is always before me. Against you, you only, have I sinned and done what is evil in your sight. Cleanse me, and I will be clean; wash me, and I will be whiter than snow. Create in me a pure heart, O God, and renew a steadfast spirit within me. Then I will teach transgressors your ways, and sinners will turn back to you.

The greatest pain in any neighbourhood is broken relationships

Trisha is a single mother who is a member of Brian and Dianne Dahl's neighbourhood group. One night there was a knock on her door, and there stood a stranger. 'Hi! You don't know me, but I live down the street. Could we talk?' She seemed so agitated that Trisha brought her in and made her a cup of coffee. Her name was Anne. 'My husband Geoff is threatening to kick me and my three kids out of the house. If that happens we will have nowhere to go. I was wondering if we might come here.'

'Well, yes, of course. But why here, why me?'

'I have been watching you and you seem like a good person.'

Trisha assured her that she was not a good person, but that God was very good. What Anne needed was Jesus in her life. They prayed together and Trisha's prayer was for reconciliation between Anne and Geoff.

Next morning, as Trisha left for work she noticed a strange car parked in the road outside her house. In the evening it was still there. Next morning it had moved into her driveway. The bonnet was up and a strange man was working on the engine.

Trisha dressed and went out to investigate. 'Excuse me, but what are you doing?'

'Fixing my car! Look, I'm sorry, but the stupid thing died on me a couple of evenings ago and I have only just found time to work on it. I'm your neighbour, by the way. I live just down there.' He pointed a greasy finger.

'You aren't Geoff, by any chance?'

'Well, yes, I am. How do you know my name?'

'Your wife Anne was over a few days ago. I understand that you two are having some problems.'

'Yeah, that about describes it. Things aren't going too smoothly for us right now. It's one thing after another. If it's not the car giving trouble, it's uncertainly at work. Sometimes it all gets too much.'

'You know what you need, don't you?'

'You tell me!'

'You need God in your life. Knowing Jesus makes all the difference to me. I know the pain of a broken family – and it was as much my fault as it was my husband's. But since I've found God the whole thing has changed. You know, some of us neighbours get together every week to talk about this sort of thing. You and Anne would be very welcome to come sometime.'

Two families destroyed; two mended

Trevor was not impressed when Andy and Stephanie took Leah to church with them. Yes, he remembered that she used to have some distant connections with the United Church, but Trevor thought she had got over all that by the time they got married. He should never have agreed to let that basketball hoop be set up in his lawn!

But when Leah came home and announced that she had become a Christian, something inside Trevor snapped. For better, for worse was one thing, but this was worse than worse – much worse.

'Steph, a terrible thing has happened,' sobbed Leah one evening, standing on their doorstep with her mascara streaked down her face. 'Trevor has left me!' Stephanie hugged and hugged her until she had settled down enough to let the whole story come out.

It seemed that Trevor, bitter over Leah's new faith, had run off with Elaine, another neighbour from the cul-de-sac. Two households in one street, destroyed. If Jesus being big in the neighbourhood was supposed to bring reconciliation, it certainly didn't feel like it. In fact it was more like a sword.

The whole community was shocked. Leah was devastated. The neighbourhood group surrounded her and the children with love and care. They prayed. They waited. They encouraged. But neither Trevor nor Elaine returned. For two years Leah waited. But then came an unexpected encouragement: impressed by the way in which Leah was bearing up, her sister started to come with her and Andy and Stephanie to church. There she also found Jesus.

Grant was taking a course in parenting skills. His wife had left him with three sons to bring up, so urgent help was needed to equip him to fill the roles of both father and mother. There he met Leah, a young woman in similar circumstances to his own.

'Do you know what has made an enormous difference to me?' she asked him one day as they both shovelled coins into a drinks machine at the college. 'God. I don't know what I would have done without knowing that he loves me. The sense of rejection by Trevor is beyond words, yet to know that I am still loved by my heavenly Father is . . . Well, it makes all the difference in the world.'

Next Sunday, Grant came to church with Leah, her sister and Andy and Stephanie. There Grant found Jesus. And the following week he was back with his three sons. Six months later Grant and Leah were married and still live in the same house on the opposite side of the cul-de-sac from Andy and Stephanie, the house with the other basket-ball hoop.

Jesus is big in that neighbourhood.

Repentance in the neighbourhood is the greatest cure for the greatest pain

Perhaps the most intimate environment for fostering repentance is the neighbourhood group. A congregation reciting together the General Confession is not as close to home as a dozen neighbours expressing repentance in a living-room.

In one neighbours' group I was leading we studied the miracle of the healing of the woman with the internal haemorrhage. Discussion nibbled at the question of why the woman was so secretive about her approach to Jesus. Why did she want to touch the hem of his cloak, then melt incognito into the crowd?

Vi, who is quiet and withdrawn and rarely says anything, suggested that perhaps she didn't want to bother Jesus when he was busy with other more important matters.

'I don't think that was why it was at all!' retorted Nancy. 'If I had an embarrassing personal problem like that, I wouldn't announce it publicly to the whole village. It beats me why we put up with all the ads on the TV about feminine hygiene.'

'Do you suppose she was ashamed of something?'

'Yes. I wonder how the problem started. It says that she had been bleeding for twelve years.'

'That's interesting. It also records the age of the

little daughter of Jairus, whom Jesus was hurrying to heal. She was twelve, too. So she must have been born around the same time as the lady's problem started.'

'Do you think the lady had a back-street abortion that may have damaged her in some way?'

'Oh, come off it! Let's not always drag the abortion issue into everything!'

'Yes, but if Jesus knows everything and he knew that she was just being discreet over a matter of personal hygiene, why did he publicly embarrass her?'

'I think it must have been that she was ashamed of something and Jesus knew that it was important for her to have the opportunity to confess it, to make a clean breast of it. That way she could be pronounced clean before the whole community, putting an end to all further gossip.'

At the end of a lively discussion I suggested that there might be issues that we too needed to confess to each other. It took a little time to get things moving. I started off by sharing something I was ashamed of and asked the others to pray for me in this matter. One or two of the others came out with things that were on their hearts.

Then Ralph, who had been the one to suggest that maybe there was something that the lady was ashamed of, cleared his throat. 'I have something that I'd like to share.' It was immediately apparent that he was on the edge of tears. No one breathed as he gathered the courage to come out with it.

'I don't know how to tell you this. In fact I have never told anyone about it. Three years ago I got

Jane to have an abortion.' He choked and it took a while before he could continue. Gary, who was next to him, put an arm round his shoulders. 'At the time it seemed so sensible. Amanda was still in nappies and not sleeping well at night. Jane was attending night school and I had pressure at work. There was no way we could take on the load of an extra child. But ever since then I have carried this around with me. Amanda should have a two-year-old little brother or sister by now, but I killed it. Jane and I have grown apart over the issue. I just can't carry it alone any more. Will you ask God to forgive me?'

We did, there and then.

That opened the flood gates for others to follow. That neighbours' group was never the same after that. We knew the worst about each other and loved each other all the more because of it.

A few weeks later Louis joined the group. He was a taxi driver of Spanish origin, so it was surprising that he remained silent for the first three weeks he attended. He appeared ill at ease and slipped away quickly as soon as the discussion was ended.

But the fourth week was different. After the last 'Amen' was over we sat there for a respectable pause, so as not to look too eager to grab another coffee. Anne was just getting up to put the kettle on again when Louis spoke. 'Just a minute. Before you go I have to get something off my chest.' We all subsided into our chairs. 'I have enjoyed these neighbourhood meetings over the past few weeks since I started coming, but at the same time they make me very uncomfortable. I believe in God and all this stuff in the Bible, but the more I read it, the more I feel unclean. I haven't lived a very good life. There are many people I have wronged and somehow that gets between me and God. I know he doesn't like it.' Then he turned to Boomer, my next-door neighbour. 'Boomer, can you remember a fellow coming into your shop a couple of years ago? He disagreed with the amount you were charging and so he pushed your tool box over?'

'You bet I do! The maniac even started to attack me. We called the police in the end. The lads still talk about it.' We all laughed.

Louis didn't. The laughter died in our throats. 'Boomer, don't you recognise me? That was me. I want to ask you to forgive me. I am very sorry.'

Repentance, like faith, is better caught than taught.

God's forgiveness is big enough to hold a whole nation together

Probably the greatest pain that people suffer is the pain of broken relationships. It seems that everywhere we turn people are broken, families are broken, neighbourhoods are broken, even whole countries are broken.

It is as Ambassadors of Reconciliation that some of us set off across Canada on that five-year pilgrimage of reconciliation. Canada prides itself on being a mosaic of peoples, cultures and beliefs. But the mosaic is breaking up. Is the forgiveness of God big and strong enough to encompass a whole nation?

Certainly, but it operates from the grassroots, one person at a time.

Northern Ireland has been a divided country with cracks of brokenness extending back into a long history of pain. I was speaking at a meeting in Belfast a few years ago. At the back of the hall was a man in his thirties, selling books. When the event was over and most people had already left, I got into conversation with him. He hadn't always sold books for a living. He had been a policeman until he had been retired from the force for health reasons.

I probed.

'Well, Justyn, it all started one day when I was off duty and driving through Belfast with my two boys sitting in the back seat. I drew up at some traffic lights, and alongside me pulled this rusty estate car. Sitting in the front were two fellows whom I half recognised. I saw a lot of people in my job, you understand. Well, the driver wound down his window, pointed a gun at my face and squeezed the trigger. Next thing I knew I was in hospital. The shot had shattered my skull, but somehow missed the vital ingredients of my brain. So, you see, since then I haven't been one hundred per cent fit.'

'How did your kids react?'

'They had nightmares for weeks, but they are getting over it now.'

'What about the men who shot you? Were they arrested?'

'Well, I know who they were, right enough. But it's just my word against theirs. That's not good enough to make charges stick.'

'So they are still at large?'

'That's the extent of it.'

'But how do you feel about that? You have lost your health, your job, not to mention the suffering of your family. And they walk free.'

A great smile spread over Steve's face. 'Justyn, I have a wonderful heavenly Father who has freely forgiven me for all my sin. How could I not forgive those fellows? I fully forgive them and I hold no grudge.'

Wow! That is how you fix a broken country, one person at a time.

God's forgiveness spreads to one person at a time

Lumby is a small logging community in the interior of British Columbia. Fifteen hundred inhabitants centre their lives around a flashing traffic light at the intersection which divides the grocery store and the Bank of Commerce, the bakery and the bar. It was right by that flashing light that we set up the Band Wagon, the mobile theatre which we were dragging across Canada on our pilgrimage for reconciliation. Half the population showed up to see this strange phenomenon which had settled like an alien spaceship in the heart of their community.

The music started, and more were drawn in by the rock and roll sounds. Then Russ introduced us and our reason for being in Lumby.

'Cut the God crap. Just give us the tunes!' shouted a woman.

The Band Wagon provided 300 seats arranged in a horseshoe, so half the crowd faced the other half. On the one side sat a young husband and on the other sat his wife and children. It's hard to get away when you live in a small community.

'There is nothing wrong with this community,' shouted a logger. 'We don't need any help, from God or anybody else.' The broken family sat and looked at each other over the unbridgeable divide.

On the fifth and final night we were there, the place was packed. 'God will heal our land,' we proclaimed. 'But it starts in each individual heart. One Canadian at a time, one family at a time, one neighbourhood at a time, one town at a time . . . And tonight it starts with me. I repent of my selfishness which has divided me from those around me and from God my Father. I trust in the blood of Jesus to heal me. Who will join me?'

There was a line-up of people wanting to express their heartfelt repentance by being baptised. Both pastors from the churches in town were there, baptising people until their backs ached.

Kathy came to the tank, holding two small children. She turned and passed them to a poker-faced man beside her, who I took to be her husband. 'I want to be baptised,' she said. 'Things aren't easy at home and I want God to start the work of reconciliation in me. I repent of my selfishness.'

It must have been half an hour later when Al arrived at the tub. I recognised him at once as the one who had stood back while Kathy was baptised.

'I want to be baptised. I'm Kathy's husband,' he mumbled.

When he was in the tub, sitting on the side in preparation for the plunge, his voice grew a little stronger. 'I haven't made things very easy at home. In fact I don't think I have been very nice to live with. I was wounded in the Gulf war and still have the shrapnel in my back to prove it. Since then I have felt bitter and angry with everyone, not just with those who wounded me. I hate feeling like this. But if God could forgive me and take this anger away, perhaps . . .' His voice trailed off in the uncertainty of his hope.

Al was baptised, shrapnel and all. Kathy hugged him as he came out of the tub. Norm, his next-door neighbour, invited him to join his brand-new neighbours' group that he was starting next week. The whole community witnessed repentance and forgiveness in Jesus' name, healing broken relationships. And Canada was one step closer to reconciliation.

14

Tying the Knot

Confessing and baptising in Jesus' name is a sign that he lives with us

If you believe in your heart that God raised him from the dead . . . and confess with your mouth, 'Jesus is Lord' . . . you will be saved.

Repent and be baptised, every one of you, in the name of Jesus Christ, for the forgiveness of your sins.

Some fall in love, but most of us grow into it.

I first set eyes on Joy when I was just thirteen. I vividly recall sitting down with a crowd of friends at a long table in a restaurant and there opposite me at my end of the table was a stunningly beautiful girl. I was completely taken off guard. Why was I suddenly so self-conscious? I suppose it was love and I was falling into it. Gradually we became friends, but it was four anxious years before I found the courage to admit my feelings to Joy, and then only by correspondence.

I was away at college, and wrote her a letter. One endless week later I received a non-committal reply. So then I was forced to wait until the following spring before I had the opportunity to talk to her. While out in the car I finally got up the nerve: 'So, you got my letter?'

'Why did you write it?'

'I don't know. I suppose because it is true.'

'It's true for me too,' she said quietly.

Two days later I put Joy on a train back to Birmingham where she worked. We first kissed as the train lurched into motion.

Yet our relationship was still secret and it wasn't until I had just turned twenty that we officially came out of the closet. The ring I purchased was so expensive that I had to sell my car to pay for it, but the sacrifice seemed trifling. On top of the white cliffs of Beachy Head I proposed marriage, and eighteen months later we were married. Two hundred of our friends and family came to the church and listened as we formally exchanged vows. Then we all went and feasted in celebration of a sealed contract.

Introducing Fred to Jesus is like a love affair

The day will come when Fred will make the big commitment with Jesus. But the likelihood is that much time will pass before he is ready to do so; the awkward days of first meeting Jesus; the secret prayers in the night which, in the morning light, Fred may feel ashamed of having uttered. The day will come when Fred will talk straight to Jesus, seriously discussing the growing nature of his love. But how long will it then take Fred to come out of the closet and openly verbalise his confession of Jesus as his Saviour and Lord? Maybe minutes, perhaps days or even weeks. By this time any question of sacrifice will seem trifling in comparison with gaining Jesus. But finally, as the climax to the development of the relationship, Fred will invite all his friends and family to hear him officially verbalise his eternal commitment to Jesus. They will watch him take the sacramental step of baptism as he symbolises the commitment of his whole self – body, mind and spirit – to Jesus in love and faith.

So, you see, the job of introducing Fred to Jesus is a love affair.

How long do relationships take to grow?

Some are slow ...

Relationships grow in as many different ways as there are people.

Thomas, the disciple of Jesus, was terribly slow off the mark. For three years he followed Jesus, learning to love him, appreciating his wisdom, thrilling at his miracles. But he was timid, afraid of believing something about Jesus just because he wanted to believe it. It had to be unmistakably true as well as dazzlingly attractive before he would make the big commitment. When Jesus rose from the

dead and showed himself to his disciples, Thomas
was absent. Stubbornly he insisted on his right to
be a sceptic. 'Just because every fibre in my being
wants to believe he lives, that doesn't mean he really
does live. I won't believe until I experience him for
myself.' One week later Thomas was confronted by
Jesus in person. His heart was now free to rejoice
in that for which he had hardly permitted himself to
hope. And immediately he confessed with his mouth
that Jesus was Lord: 'My Lord and my God!'

'If you believe in your heart that God raised him
from the dead . . . and confess with your mouth,
"Jesus is Lord" . . . you will be saved.' It took
Thomas three years for the heart belief to grow
strong enough for his mouth to confess it.

Some grow fast

The thief who was crucified on the cross next to
Jesus, however, was a little quicker off the mark.
And for good reason, for he only had hours left to
live. Jesus' next-door neighbour on the other side
was a hard case who showed little regard for man
or God. 'If you really are the Christ,' he sneered,
'then do something Christ-like! Save your own hide
– and ours!'

'Don't you have any respect for God,' retorted
the first thief, 'since you and he are experiencing
the same sentence? We are getting just what we
deserve, but this man hasn't put a foot wrong.' To
confess God to be just and to confess himself a sinner
was his first step out of the closet.

Then he turned to Jesus: 'Jesus, remember me

when you come into your kingdom.' He made it personal – 'remember *me*' – and he confessed Jesus to be Lord, a King with a kingdom; and he clearly anticipated that God would raise Jesus from the dead, for how else would he come into his kingdom?

Belief in his heart happened almost instantaneously, followed a few seconds later by verbal confession. He never had the opportunity to formalise the commitment by baptism: baptism is inconvenient at the best of times, but when you're hanging from a ten-foot pole it's just plain awkward. And in any case baptism is but a symbol of being crucified with Jesus, and since he was doing the whole thing for real, what use had he for symbols?

Another man who moved from cynic to wholehearted believer in minutes was the jailer in the city of Philippi. 'What must I do to be saved?' he asked Paul and Silas, his prisoners. Of course a 7.5-strength earthquake helped speed up the process. Paul, who had to that point passed an uncomfortable night in the jailer's hospitality, could easily have come back with a smart-alec response. 'Nothing, stupid! There is nothing you or anyone else can do to be saved, unless you can achieve perfection, that is. No, only Jesus can save people.' But Paul was more gracious: 'Believe on the Lord Jesus to do the saving. You'll be saved OK.'

What did the jailer do? He changed his negative attitude double quick. He changed his faith from agnostic to believer in seconds. He was baptised, formalising his new relationship with Jesus. He was filled with joy. And all that before breakfast next morning.

Answering the question: 'What must I do to be saved?'

So what will happen when one day soon Fred suddenly asks you: 'How can I become a Christian? What must I do to be saved?' You could come back with a mouthful of smart-alec theology, or you could assure him that Jesus will save him and that he might as well relax and enjoy the ride.

There are many simple ways of answering his question. Here is one that I find easy to remember and simple to explain. Let me imagine a conversation, picking it up from the point where Fred has said: 'OK. I want to become a Christian. Tell me how.'

'Basically, Fred, becoming a Christian is as simple as ABC. A: Admit that you have offended God and your fellow man and ask God to get rid of your sin. Are you willing to do that, Fred?'

'No problem there. I am all too aware of my shortcomings. So what's next?'

'B: Believe the truth about Jesus, that he is God, that he not only died for the forgiveness of your sins, but is risen and alive now. Do you believe that, Fred?'

'Yes, I do believe that Jesus died and rose again for me.'

'C: Confess Jesus as Lord. It is with your mouth that you steer the course of your life. In a marriage ceremony, for example, the minister will ask the couple if they are willing to marry each other. They will respond out loud, in front of witnesses: "I will."

Those words set the course for the rest of their lives. So I ask you, Fred. Do you confess Jesus Christ as Lord? If you do, say: "I confess Jesus Christ as Lord."'

'I confess Jesus Christ as Lord.'

At that point we could shout hallelujah, for really he has expressed his openness to God to do the rest. However, I usually make it more special by inviting the person to turn all that into a prayer, so he can express it to God himself, rather than to me. I may lead him phrase by phrase in a prayer, or I may pray first and then invite him to make his own prayer. The kind of prayer I would lead in is like this:

> God, I do admit that I have sinned and I ask you to forgive me and to take it all away. I believe that Jesus is your Son, that he died for me and is now risen. And I do confess, here and now, that Jesus is Lord.

There is lots of theology that is not covered in that simple ABC outline, but it's only a step. And in any case it's not the knowledge of the theology that saves the person: it's the truth of the theology. It is the blood of Jesus that cleanses him from sin, whether he understands it at the time or not. It is the Holy Spirit who comes into his life and baptises him with the presence of God, even if he doesn't understand the Trinity. He is born again, even if he has never heard the term. Jesus takes care of all those details, for it's Jesus who does the saving.

Does God do it right there and then? That is entirely up to God. Your confidence and Fred's is that he is faithful and will keep all his promises one by one. But all the promises of God find their 'Yes' in Jesus and Fred has said 'Yes' in the name of Jesus.

Some people need a nudge

Some people are a little slow at making up their minds and may need a small kick in the backside to get them motivated. Ingrid is a habitual procrastinator. Actually it may be that she is a perfectionist who insists on knowing all about everything, covering each possible option before she feels qualified to make an intelligent decision. The decision to accept Kevin's proposal of marriage was therefore terribly hard. After all, there were roughly five million other eligible bachelors in Canada, and how was she ever to know all there was to know about each of them so that she could arrive at an informed decision? Yes, she loved Kevin dearly, but with so many other possibilities could she really be sure she was making the right decision? Kevin insisted that it was a choice based on what she knew of him. 'Do you love me?' he asked.

'Yes, of course. You know I do.'

'Then will you marry me?'

'I'd like to, but I just don't know how to make up my mind. What if I change my mind tomorrow? That would be awful!'

So Kevin resolved to give Ingrid an appropriate nudge in the you-know-where. He purchased the ring and a bouquet of flowers. During choir practice one evening, he walked out in front of the whole hundred-strong choir and called Ingrid out. Then, getting down on one knee in front of her, he produced the ring and the flowers and he asked her to marry him. How could she refuse?

Daniel Cozens is a colourful Anglican evangelist working in the United Kingdom. He started life as an artist and found Jesus in his twenties. So excited is he by his discovery that he has never shut up about it since! He has a disarming directness that some find offensive but most find refreshing. I was working with him as part of a team he was leading in Jersey, in the Channel Islands. To one of the meetings were dragged three unwilling husbands of wives who had been Christians for some time. These three husbands had never quite got round to following the good example of their wives. They were in need of a small kick in the posterior. They stuck it out through the service and at the end headed out of the side door of the church for a smoke. That was where Daniel found them. 'Good evening, gentlemen. I take it that you are not yet Christians. Why not?'

They shuffled their feet and shilly-shallied. One said: 'Well, no special reason really. We just haven't made up our minds yet.'

'Am I right in thinking that your wife is a Christian?' Daniel challenged.

'Yeah, that's right. Turned religious about three years ago,' one man replied.

'Do you notice any changes in her?'

'Could say that. She's nicer to the kids. She packed in smoking. Goes to church a lot, that kind of thing.'

'Overall a change for the better, would you say?'
'Yeah.'

'And you've had three years to think about it.'
Dan paused for effect, stroking his chin. 'Is there
any reason why you shouldn't become Christians
right now?' he asked all three of them.

'Well, we'd need some time to think about it.'

'You've had three years! Tell you what. I'll give
you three more minutes to think about it. Then if
you don't come up with good reasons not to become
Christians – well, let's get on with it.' With that
he pulled the sleeve of his coat up his arm, laying
bare his wristwatch, and stood there looking at it
for three minutes while the three men smoked and
squirmed!

'Time is up! You fellows have had years to think
about it, seeing the example of your wives. The time
has come to choose. What's the answer going to be?
Yes or no?'

Now that's what I call a good, well-aimed kick.
I'm not sure I would have the guts for quite so direct
an approach. But coming from Daniel it seemed quite
natural.

Letting the preacher deliver the nudge

Billy Graham has called more people to make up
their minds than any other person ever. At the end of
a crusade meeting he would say: 'Tonight I'm going
to ask you to get up out of your seat and come to
the front to receive Christ.' Then, as the choir sings
'Just as I am', thousands of people respond. Why?

Because it gives the person a definite opportunity to take definite action. 'Tonight' – that's *now*. 'I'm going to ask you' – that's *me*. 'To get up out of your seat and come to the front' – *I know where that is*. 'To receive Christ' – *that's just what I want to do, but never quite knew how*. The worshipful accompaniment helps. The thousands of others walking the same direction also help. The expectation that may have been built up over previous exposure to Billy Graham's ministry may also help. The prompting of the Holy Spirit, who whispers, 'Today, if you hear his voice, harden not your heart,' is irresistible.

I have heard people express reservations about preachers calling for a definite, on-the-spot response. However, there is much in the Bible to support such a call. 'Choose this day whom you will serve.' 'How long will you go limping between two different opinions?' 'God now commands all men everywhere to repent.'

It is important to see the altar call in the right context. The people who attend such meetings will probably have been in the process of getting to know Jesus for years. This is not a call in isolation. It is the end of a long process that the Lord Jesus himself has been orchestrating.

Delivering the nudge personally

I'm a preacher myself, but I hesitate to be too direct when face to face with a friend. So I invite my neighbours to come with me to hear someone else preach the gospel.

But that may be a coward's way out. Would this be too embarrassing . . . ?

'Fred, I know that you believe in God and that you pray. But have you ever asked Jesus to make you a real Christian?'

'Fred, the turning point in my life was the day I asked God to forgive my sins and to make me a Christian. I hope you don't mind my asking, but have you ever done that?'

Freda was a slow developer, a life-long procrastinator who at age eighty-six still hadn't deliberately received Jesus. I knew her before we emigrated to Canada, and so on a visit back home to England I called into the old people's home where she lived and offered to take her out for a drive. She was thrilled to accept and off we went.

'Freda, I want to show you the house where I lived when I was a child.' Actually it was a mansion which had been converted into a Christian conference centre. My parents had run it and so I grew up with the run of a hundred-acre estate. Freda was impressed. Then I drove her slowly down the long tree-lined driveway and pulled over as close as I could to a huge redwood tree. 'Freda, it was beside that tree that I made the most significant decision in my entire life. Can I tell you about it?'

'Oh yes, dear. Please do.'

'My sister and I used to go to Sunday School in the village over there. I hated it, for it took place on a Sunday afternoon and that seemed to ruin the whole day. To make matters worse, my mother was Scottish and insisted that I wear a kilt, so I was always the only one wearing a skirt on my side of the aisle.

'One day the lesson was on that verse in the Bible where Jesus says: "I stand at the door and knock. If anyone hears my voice and opens the door, I will come in." The teacher showed us a print of the famous painting that hangs in St Paul's Cathedral of Jesus standing at the door knocking. "All you have to do is invite him to come in," he told us. Then we learned a chorus that went: "Into my heart, Into my heart, Come into my heart, Lord Jesus. Come in today, Come in to stay, Come into my heart, Lord Jesus."

'Well, on the way home that day, my sister and I walked together up this drive here. She was worried that I was being too slow in making up my mind to become a Christian, so she bullied me a little. "You are not a real Christian, Justyn, because you have never asked Jesus to come into your life. So don't you think it's time to ask him today?" I was only six years old, so she might have been a little more patient! But I said OK.

'We turned off the drive right here where we are sitting and went up to that big tree. "How do I ask him to come in? I don't know what to say," I must have asked. So she prompted me and together we repeated the words of that chorus: "Into my heart, Into my heart, Come into my heart, Lord Jesus. Come in today, Come in to stay, Come into my heart, Lord Jesus."

'Do you know, Freda, Jesus came in on that very day and has never left me since. It was the greatest day of my life.'

'That's really nice, dear. Thank you for telling me.'

'That's OK. Freda, can I ask you: have you ever asked Jesus to come into your life?'

She looked sad for a moment. 'No, dear, I never quite did.'

'Well, would you like to ask him to come in right here and now?'

'Could I? But I don't know what to say.'

So I told her and together we said the words: "Into my heart, Into my heart, Come into my heart, Lord Jesus. Come in today, Come in to stay, Come into my heart, Lord Jesus."

I procrastinated until I was six years old, and thank God for my sister Jennifer, who kicked my backside, for I had waited far too long! Freda waited until she was eighty-six, and thank God that I kicked her backside, otherwise she might still be dragging her heels.

Some people just need reminding of what they already have

Bill was a member of our neighbourhood group. We used John's Gospel as the basis for our discussions. 'Why did no one ever tell me this stuff?' he complained after a couple of weeks. 'I used to go to church, but no one ever brought all this up.'

We got right through John's Gospel, to the end of chapter 20. We focused on the verse that says: 'Jesus did many other miraculous signs in the presence of his disciples, which are not recorded in this book. But these are written that you may believe that Jesus is the Christ, the Son of God, and that by believing you may have life in his name.'

'We have made a careful study of the things written in this book. The object of the book, according to this paragraph, is to give us the kind of faith in Jesus, the Son of God, that will result in our having life in his name, or being born again.' I turned to the person next to me. I knew where her faith rested, but I asked anyway: 'Amanda. Do you have everlasting life? Are you a real Christian?'

'Yes, I do have life. That life is in Jesus and I know I have him.'

Then I looked at Bill. I had no idea where Bill stood, but he had started to pray from time to time at the end of the discussions. 'Bill, how about you? Do you have everlasting life?'

'Well, I'm not sure, really. I would like to . . .'

'Would you mind if I asked you three or four questions, Bill?'

'By all means, Justyn. Ask away!'

'Bill, are you repentant for your sin? In other words, do you turn from selfishness to God's way?'

'Yes. I wouldn't be here if I didn't want to get my life straightened out.'

'Bill, do you believe that Jesus is God, the Son of God?'

'Yes, I do now, after all these studies. That's exactly who he was.'

'And do you believe that having been crucified for your sins, he rose again and is alive today?'

'Yes, I believe that. We'd hardly be praying to him if he were not alive!'

'Bill, are you open to the Holy Spirit taking over your life?'

'Yes, I'd like that.'

'Then, Bill, if this is true, will you make this confession: "I confess that Jesus Christ is Lord"?'

'No problem. I confess that Jesus Christ is Lord.'

'Bill, the Bible assures you that you have everlasting life, you are an heir of his holiness, you are a child of God.' I showed him where.

A huge smile spread over his face, like the sun rising in the morning. It was relief, understanding, joy all rolled into one. Bill and Jesus were out of the closet. Their relationship was official.

Some people need to unblock the dam between their heart and their mouth

I was speaking at a youth meeting of the Keswick Convention in the north of England. Keswick is a beautiful old-world town with slate-roofed houses fronting right on to the streets, little alleyways beckoning you back into history, market squares and a park with a river flowing through it. The mountains, rounded by the wind, stand guard over the town, and the rain still lashes down even in July – maybe especially in July, when thousands of Christians go there for a two-week Bible convention. After the meeting I grabbed some good old fish and chips soaked in vinegar and headed for a sheltered bench in the park. A young man walking by recognised me as the speaker from the previous meeting.

'Hey, Justyn, I've got a question I wanted to

ask you, but there were too many people in the convention tent. Mind if I sit down for a moment?'

'Be my guest.' I offered him a soggy chip.

'Justyn, I agree with everything you said, but I just can't know it. How can I be sure that it is all true?'

He told me about his connection to a Baptist church. Yes, he had asked Jesus into his life on at least three occasions. Had he come in? Well that was the problem. How was he to know?

'Monty,' – that was his name – 'your certainty is based solely on what he promises.'

'But it's so hard to go on with no real evidence. I don't even feel like he has come in.'

We talked until all my chips were cold. The birds had a feast. I couldn't sort out his problem. So I suggested we should pray together about it, asking God why Monty felt nothing. When I had said my piece: 'Now Monty, you pray. Tell the Lord what you do believe and lay your questions before him.'

There was a long silence. 'Monty, aren't you going to pray?'

'I am praying.'

'Well, don't cut me out of the conversation. Pray out loud, so I can join in with you.'

'Oh, no! I never pray out loud. Prayer is a personal matter, just between me and God.'

'Have you ever prayed aloud?'

'No, I don't think I ever have. Except for set prayers in church when we all pray together.'

'Well, pray out loud now. There is no one to overhear us, only God.'

So Monty started to pray in a rather self-conscious

manner. He mumbled a bit about his problems of believing, but then he included some kind of statement of faith, telling God what he did believe. Among the things he said was a confession of Jesus as God. Almost immediately he broke down and wept. Through his sobs he choked out: 'It's OK now, Justyn. I know it's true. Thank you.'

It's hard to analyse Monty's feelings, but if you ask me the belief in his heart had been there for some time. But there it had remained, like a river that is blocked up with nowhere to flow. A river like that becomes stagnant. Simply taking the next step of confessing that Jesus is Lord had unblocked the dam. Sometimes we can help people to know Jesus by taking them by the hand and leading them on to the next step.

Some people come to it naturally with no prompting

Boomer was our neighbour over the street who refused the invitation to the evangelistic crusade but who readily accepted the invitation when invited to join a neighbourhood group. He joined in October. Just before Christmas he first prayed aloud, a halting, nervous kind of a prayer. By the end of January he was praying confidently and, taking my lead, he concluded by calling on the name of the Lord: '. . . in the name of the Lord Jesus Christ.'

I know and he knows that he was not a Christian when first he came to the group. And we both knew that by January he was a Christian. Just when he crossed over neither one of us knows. But somewhere in heaven the recording angel made an entry in the Lamb's book of life and a celestial party erupted.

'Can you explain to me why my mouth has changed?' he asked me one day. 'I used to be able to curse a person up one wall and down the other. Now I can't even stand hearing others do it. What is happening?'

'It's simple, Boomer. The Bible says that the tongue is like a rudder on a ship or a bit in the mouth of a horse. If you can control the bit, the whole horse will change direction, and likewise with a rudder and a ship. Human tongues are the most uncontrollable part of our body, described in the Bible as being like a snake, a monster full of deadly venom.'

'That's my mouth, all right,' agreed Boomer.

'But when the Holy Spirit comes into a person the first thing he takes control of is the rudder, the bit – your tongue. For as soon as he gains control of your tongue he can redirect your whole body. Not only are you refraining from saying blasphemous things, but now you are saying fundamentally good things. You now call Jesus Lord. That is the first indicator that the Holy Spirit has taken over the helm of your life. Just you watch the rest of your life change direction!' And we all watched fascinated as the girlie pictures came down in his office; as his business ethics changed; as his attitude towards his family mellowed.

I told him that the next step forward was to be baptised. He wasn't too sure about that at first. He wasn't a churchy kind of guy.

'You don't have to be baptised in a church building,' I assured him. 'We could borrow someone's swimming pool or rent a hot tub and do it in your home.'

Boomer thought about it for a while. In the middle of December he made up his mind. 'Justyn, I want to be baptised and I would like you to baptise me.'

'Fine,' I agreed. 'When and where?'

'Well, I have lived most of my life connected in some way or other to the waterfront in White Rock. So I thought it would be nice to be baptised in the ocean, by the pier.'

'That's fine with me. But we'll have to wait several months before the water gets warm enough.'

'I don't want to wait. I thought Christmas Eve would be a good day. Besides, I've got a wet suit.'

Two weeks wasn't much notice, so we swung into action. First we held a meeting of the neighbourhood group. How could we make the very most of the occasion? Boomer drew up a list of everyone with whom he had any contact: friends, family, people at work, tradespeople, doctor, dentist, old schoolmates . . . the list went on and on.

We booked a whole restaurant right opposite the pier. They agreed to lay on a buffet reception for Boomer and friends. They also had a convenient washroom that we could use to change out of our wet things.

Next we printed a special invitation which resembled a wedding invitation. We wanted it to look official and special, for it would be a very important day. This is it:

You are invited to
the Baptism of
Dan (Boomer) Saunders
at 1 p.m. on Sunday 24th December 1989
to take place by the White Rock Pier
and afterwards for a light luncheon at
Kelly's Bistro
(on Marine Drive above the Pier)

Someone wrote a press release and sent it to all the local media.

The true spirit of Christmas

There are many ways of celebrating Christmas, but few are as unusual as an event to take place on Christmas Eve on White Rock beach. A Baptism.

Dan (Boomer) Saunders, known to many as the Exhaust King of Marine Drive, is taking the plunge, literally. At 1 p.m. he will enter the sea for a total immersion type of baptism.

'Christmas is the birthday of Jesus and I want to celebrate it in the most meaningful way I know how,' says Boomer. 'When Jesus was born in Bethlehem there was no room for him except in a stable. I haven't given him much room in my life up until now, either, but I want him to be born in me and to live his life through me from now on. What's more. I want everyone to know that I am not ashamed to associate myself with him publicly on his birthday, or any other day come to that. On the day of his death he associated with me in a rather embarrassing manner, so if I feel a little embarrassment on Sunday, it won't be at all a bad thing.'

Justyn Rees is to perform the baptism. 'Of course I'm going to wear a wet suit. I'm no polar bear! I admire Boomer's courage, not just to brave the cold but to be baptised openly. Most people keep their Christianity hidden away in church where only the very religious will see it. Boomer grew up on the waterfront and for him to be openly baptised by the pier is most meaningful.'

Spectators are welcome and those wanting to sing carols are also invited to be at the pier at 1 p.m. on Christmas Eve.

The day dawned, bright, clear and crisp. We arrived half an hour early and members of the neighbourhood group started to sing Christmas carols. By the time 1 o'clock came there was a crowd of at least a couple of hundred. A TV camera crew was there, anxious to capture the spirit of Christmas for the viewers. The local member of parliament was there. Santa had been passing, so he stopped to see what was going on. Someone had brought a tank of helium and was handing out balloons. The crowd stood along the pier and the shoreline, forming a natural amphitheatre as Boomer and I waded out into the glass-flat sea. The sun danced and sparkled over the water and the seagulls flew up and circled overhead.

'Ladies and gentlemen,' I started. 'Today is the birthday of Jesus Christ who came to earth to a stable two thousand years ago. And today we are to celebrate the fact that Dan Saunders has been reborn as Jesus has come to live in him. Boomer, tell us about it.'

Boomer told how he had become a Christian. Then I invited anyone in the crowd to shout out something of encouragement.

Among the various and often amusing things that were shouted were two very significant comments. One was from an older lady with grey hair and a radiant face. I recognised Cathie Macaulay as a Faith Missionary. For years she had been involved in evangelistic work here in White Rock. The form of her evangelism was as traditional as it comes. She would stand in uniform, shouting through a loud-hailer and singing hymns accompanied by an ancient treadle organ. The local council had finally closed her down the previous summer. She had done it for years, and when Boomer was a teenager he used to make it his Sunday afternoon sport to heckle and give her a hard time. But Cathie recognised such behaviour as an appeal to be prayed for. And pray she had.

Her voice came clearly over the water that day: 'Dan, I want you to know that I'm still praying for you.'

Next was John Clarke. John was a local pastor who had started his ministry twenty years previously as a youth evangelist working the beach at White Rock. Among other contacts had been a teenage terror that everyone called Boomer. On one occasion John even persuaded this young rebel to come with him to a Christian camp. So obnoxious had Boomer's behaviour been that he had had to be sent home. Yet John had prayed on.

John's comment to Boomer that Christmas Eve was a little less spiritual than Cathie's, and the meaning was lost on the crowd. But Boomer understood. 'Boomer, I have waited for this for twenty years! What kept you so long?'

We prayed, and then I lowered Boomer under the water, all six foot six of him. The crowd on the shore saw the pinks and mauves and orange reflections of the sun ripple outwards, and the seagulls swooped down low to see if any fish were rising.